The Magic of an Upper Peninsula Autumn

Photos and Commentary

by
Bob Collins

Southern Arizona Press

The stunning Lake of the Clouds Overlook;
Porcupine Mountains State Park, early October of 2018

The Magic of an Upper Peninsula Autumn

Photos and Commentary

by
Bob Collins

The Magic of an Upper Peninsula Autumn

By Bob Collins

First Edition

Author: Bob Collins
Editor: Paul Gilliland
Formatting: Southern Arizona Press
All Photography: Bob Collins

Published by Southern Arizona Press
Sierra Vista, Arizona 85635
www.SouthernArizonaPress.com

ISBN: 978-1-960038-28-9

Photography and Commentary

Contents

About the Title

No doubt, the majority of this book is about the power of autumn in Michigan's Upper Peninsula (the UP). But, I do "sneak in" a couple of scenic gems in far-northern Wisconsin as well. So, I could have expanded the title to something like..."The Magic of an Upper Peninsula Autumn (with a Touch of Northern Wisconsin Thrown in)".

Though, I trust that you - the reader - will understand the need for the shorter title and forgive me for doing so.

About the Author

I am now in my mid-50s, and for almost 30 years was a bank courier and did similar work elsewhere; but during that time, have also had a deep affinity for traveling, hiking, and nature photography.

Not long after graduating from the University of Illinois in Champaign, Illinois (philosophy, way back in May of 1989), I went to work on a version of that courier job - basically, moving lots of stuff around for a good, local bank, from location to location, in and around the Chicagoland area. This seemed to go hand in hand with my penchant for driving - almost an addiction, you might say.

Not long after, a late-autumn trip to Arizona around Thanksgiving, 1990 (with my dad and brother John) kind of jump started, "opened my eyes" to real scenic splendor - part of which involved a long day trip up from Phoenix, through Sedona, culminating in Grand Canyon National Park. This effectively cemented the notion of true, scenic grandeur in my mind.

Two years later, I would take an early-July trip to Arkansas (albeit, in extreme heat!) Then, one year later - late July of '93 - I would take another "revolutionary trip", with dear friend Dom; this time, out west to Montana and Wyoming. This was even more of an eye opener to scenic grandeur - one of the colossal examples being the stunning drive over US 212, Beartooth Pass Highway, once termed by long-time CBS icon Charles Kuralt as "The most beautiful road in America."

Finally, in late July of '97, with dear friend Tony, I took a classic trip to Alaska. Talk about true grandeur! And in classic, finale fashion, part of that trip included a stunning display of the aurora borealis - out our airplane windows, on the return flight.

This was amazing as well and kind of jump started my love of nature photography. Plus, on a tip from my brother Terry, I utilized the color-saturated print film Agfa Ultra, 50 speed.

For those of you who remember the old days of shooting with film, this was kind of the mirror image of Velvia slide film - but for prints. You would get these amazing, very-saturated colors that pumped an extra level of beauty into your work. (A bit more on this in the film-technique section of the book.)

Now, bringing things right to the core of this book, in late September of '97, Tony and his girl at the time were about to take a trip to Upper Michigan. He actually wanted to borrow my old, trusted Nikon EM camera, but instead ended up borrowing another Nikon from a friend in his building - and would also utilize Agfa and Velvia on his trip.

At the time, when he said "Michigan", I must confess that I did not think much of it - not knowing much about fall colors or splendor of any kind up there. After all, only a couple months earlier, we experienced the grandeur of Alaska. So, I wasn't really thinking of other kinds at that point; was actually still in a state of awe about what we had experienced. When he got back, over a week later in early October, he showed me the prints and slides. My reaction to the colors and scenes, in short:

LITERALLY JAW DROPPING!

Yes, I almost could not believe what I was looking at: amazing colors of every variety and unique scenes of nature that were really eye popping. It was one of those stunning revelations you get as a traveler that is what I term an "original." In other words, you are almost in a state of novel euphoria about what you are viewing or have experienced. In a deep part of your mind, it seems almost unreal - like being thrown into another dimension of pleasure.

Dedications

I dedicate this book to my folks - both now physically gone, but psychologically very much with me and to my dear siblings, friends in life and social media, coworkers, and one fine CEO who headed our bank for years (Mr. Bill Conaghan) - all of whose inspiration and life experiences have helped me. Also of note are the important folks in my life who are listed at the bottom of this section, even a couple unlisted who have passed on; but whether with me now or not, they have each - in their own ways - contributed to my growth and development on the human level.

I also want to put in a special mention for a rare traveling book that my father gave me many years back - *Westward Ho: Through the Scenic West*, by Fred Bond (Cuneo Press). This 1947 travel book was years ahead of its time - as it laid out splendid scenic spots, roads, and travel tips for the western states; and even included a color-coded map in the back folder, all before the interstates were built!

To this day, in fact, I still utilize it and some of its main philosophy will be quoted later on.

I also want to put in an honorable mention for another good book from 2001, *Fall Colors Across North America*, by Anthony E. Cook, with a foreword by Art Wolfe. In this, Anthony also gives credit to Fujichrome Velvia film.

Perhaps above all, though, I dedicate this to the stunning beauty of Michigan's Upper Peninsula. Even now, after having done it 19 times in 24 years, with this actually marking the 25th (silver anniversary), it never ceases to amaze me.

In short, it has given me, very simply... some of the best, most-peaceful, visually awe-inspiring experiences of my life.

My family: John, Sue, Terry and his wife Elizabeth, Patty, Linda, and Phil; my sweetheart, Jill; cousins: here, Erin and Sean, as well as those in Tennessee, Carl, Gretta, and Sandy and elsewhere, Jeffrey and Mike R.; dear friends: Dom, and his wife Lidija in Germany, Tony; Ivica, Carlo, Magdiel, Eddy, fellow traveler Paul Day, Ulli, Darwin, Laura, Gina; the Butzens, the Wrenns, the Englunds, Tom Hearty, Jennifer Weeden; my former colleagues/friends from Bridgeview Bank and my schooling years, too numerous to mention; fellow, accomplished photographers - Phil Stagg, Lynn Funkhouser, Larry Farley, and Bill Prough; and professor of philosophy at the U of I, then Indiana U, years later - Frederick F. Schmitt. To this day, his intellect and writing style I admire a great deal, hope to have learned from. An honorable mention to the great works of Clint Eastwood and Rod Serling - whom I admire greatly; and our best cats from over the decades.

I also wanted to give special thanks to Paul Gilliland and his staff at Southern Arizona Press (www.southernarizonapress.com) for their tireless work in improving this manuscript.

Also, in the brief appendix, you can find some other sites where I have my general pictures included from these many years of traveling. Needless to say, the UP is well represented.

Navigation Instructions within the Book

As much as possible, there have been additional addresses and aids added to help with the navigation instructions within this book.

Each entry will provide as much of the following as possible to assist with locating specific places using Google Maps:

[Street address as listed in Google Maps; website address; telephone number; Military Grid Reference System (MGRS) Coordinates]

Example:

Sand Point Lighthouse [2-20 Water Plant Road, Escanaba, Michigan 49829; exploringthenorth.com; (906) 789-6790; 16TDR9655265681]

To use the MGRS Coordinates, simply type the 15-digit MGRS into the search bar of Google Maps. (Make sure you use the capital letters and do not include any spaces.)

The Power of Autumn in the Upper Peninsula

It was the prior-mentioned, initial visual jolt that would set in motion for me, many subsequent years of traveling to the UP in early autumn. Granted, I have been to many amazing places to explore and photograph over the years; e.g., Mexico, Canada, Ireland, Germany, Austria, Alaska, Hawaii, Florida, the Southeast, Northeast, Lower Michigan, and the great western mountains, but this one place seems to draw me back, time and time again.

Of course, based out of Chicago and adjacent suburbs, it is relatively easy to get to and experience - in terms of both distance and general economics. For the latter, you can still find places that are good for the pocketbook - while enjoying a great combination of land, sea, waters, sky, and colors that are about as good as it gets in the states and in my opinion, strongly rivaling that of the Northeast's classic fall gems - Vermont, New Hampshire, and adjacent states.

You essentially have a microcosm of great landscapes found in other splendid places in the country: mountains (albeit, smaller scale), deep forests, sea (primarily Lake Superior), lakes/lake reflections, and a strong lineup of waterfalls that reach from one end of the peninsula to the other. There are even a couple areas which seem like they are out of the Desert Southwest!

Plus, there are key areas in which strong displays of the aurora borealis occur. These are mostly along the Lake Superior shoreline; e.g., Pictured Rocks and the Keweenaw.

Not only this, but you can encounter many examples of wildlife: deer, fox, grouse, bald eagles, an occasional moose, etcetera. Plus, don't forget to try one of the UP's traditional taste treats - the pasty, which traces its roots back to Cornwall, England. This hearty dish is generally composed of minced pork, vegetables, potatoes, and other things you can customize - all wrapped in a fried pastry roll.

One prime example of the visual possibilities is this image - from a splendid 2012 trip with my sister Patty, also a UP admirer. The frontispiece is from 2018 and has a nice reflection, while this one from 2012 has richer colors. At this viewing point for Lake of the Clouds, if you hit it at the right time, a sea of colors unfolds below - almost putting you in a trance.

Way back in 2000, I planned an autumn trip to Washington state and one part of it included several overnights up in the stunning Enchantments - pristine mountain lakes surrounded by golden larch in early autumn (though, very difficult/strenuous to get to.) In preparation for this, I purchased another fine traveling book, by Ron C. Judd and Dan A. Nelson, titled *Pacific Northwest Hiking* (original printing, 1995; but updated since.) When discussing the power of the Enchantments, they basically referred to what I term the photographer's paradox; roughly, they said:

"The Enchantments are a photographer's dream, but also nightmare: too much to shoot, and from too many angles."

I would say the same for the UP in early autumn. For example, I often find myself having to stop, pull the vehicle over, shoot a scene; then repeat again, countless times. In some cases, I am almost NOT able to keep up - because of constantly being overwhelmed by the visual feast - the kaleidoscope of stunning colors and forms. Many of the scenes are simply sublime.

I also remember about a decade back ... I was up at the overlook above, admiring the view, along with another traveler. She said that, much like me, she is a fan of Colorado as well, and lives there - but hadn't been back to Michigan in years (having lived in the state many years before.) She then remarked, roughly ... "I am amazed at how nice this really is. Having lived in Colorado for a long time, it's a given how splendid that is, but here in Michigan, this is still quite something."

Amen.

My Favorite Fall Locations

Here, I just want to briefly expand upon some fall-color "hot spots." These are my favorite places in the country where I feel the color punch and general experience is strongest, though not necessarily in a specific order:

Utah: The variety of forms, scenes, colors, and geometry in the landscapes is almost unsurpassed, in my opinion. But come autumn, when foliage is sprinkled in as well, the entire notion of scenery is taken to its pinnacle.

Colorado: Where millions of aspens put on an amazing show of color across the mountains. In this case, you don't have the variety of colors as the UP, or the Northeast; but this is made up for by the SHEER VOLUME of aspens turning and even among these, there are subtle shades to be found.

Vermont, New Hampshire, Maine, and Northeast states: Where the magic of color variety reigns supreme. This is also where colors mix nicely with farms, churches, covered bridges, seacoasts, etc.

The UP: Where, much like the last mentioned, color variety also reigns supreme. But in this case, the UP capitalizes on NATURAL SCENES; e.g., waterfalls, rivers, lakeshores, mixed hardwoods, lake reflections, and "down-a-fall-road" scenes (more examples of this in the county sections.)

Plus, the incredible variety of hardwoods that turn amazing colors: maples, birch, aspens, oaks, larch, and sumac and in dazzling red, yellow, gold, orange, brown, even subtle shades of pink - both in and on the forest floor.

Of course, the latter area is really the focus of this book.

The Splendor of Autumn

Fall, the early part in particular, just seems to be a joyous time to be out in nature; quite frankly, to be alive. In many parts of the country, you have the best weather of the year: crisp-blue skies, temperatures from the upper 50s to low 70s, ample sunshine, cool breezes, reduced insects, more-economical lodging, and reduced crowds.

This last part I cannot stress enough.

For many years, my dear friends and I would take great trips out West in July. In 2017, we did so to the Southwest, in overwhelming heat. Granted, the July weather cycle is quite nice, reliable - with many sunny days, limited rain, and depending on location, you will have comfortable temperature ranges. Plus, of course, in the western mountains you have that cooling effect - which dents the July heat nicely.

But, in my opinion, one downside is the crowds. With many children out for summer and traditional family vacations now ensuing, you often encounter a mass of humanity.

In the summer of 2021 this was powerfully true with so many folks “breaking out” of the pandemic, and simply flooding the national parks, it had gotten to the point where officials had no choice but to turn many of them away. The same thing occurred in the prime months of 2022.

This was dramatically illustrated in some of my trips as well. In our 2012 trip to California, Yosemite National Park in particular, we went in mid-July and the entrance on the west side – Merced - was almost like a parking lot, well over a couple blocks long!

Of course, there are, unfortunately, many other examples of this: The ferry crossing to and from Washington Island (Door County, Wisconsin) and the large crowds that now gather out at Horseshoe Bend Canyon in

Arizona to name a few. There are, of course, a host of others. (I wager that many of you have now experienced some of these as well.)

In the fall, however, you experience less of these situations. The kids are back in school and many folks in general just don't take long trips anymore. Granted, there are still some crowded areas in the national parks and other scenic spots, but nothing like what occurs in the summer months. If you add in your visit to take advantage of weekdays, you will find even less in the way of crowds. Also, in the autumn, the summer smoke, which has been increasing in recent years, is pretty much gone.

Plus, in the case of the Michigan Upper Peninsula, you get those amazing fall colors which paint the landscapes with supreme beauty.

Another aspect noteworthy of commentary and that is almost beyond any words, images, or videos I can share with you: the pleasant aroma of an autumn forest after it rains.

During one UP trip a few years back, I experienced the excellence of the Piers Gorge area in this circumstance - on the Wisconsin/UP border (more on this later on.)

There are some glorious spots along the trails to observe, no question; but that aroma after a rainfall just intensified the hiking experience to another level, adding to the sensory pleasures.

So, I definitely recommend traveling more in the fall. The general advantages will reward you greatly. (And as you drive along, it goes without saying, play some of your favorite music. For many years now, my personal favorites for the soothing effects include the works of Enya and Aaron Copland; but at the other end of the spectrum, ELO as well. Ultimately, though, I am sure you have yours. There is really no right or wrong here.)

In short, look about you in every direction - side to side, toward the sky, and down; for, much as in life itself, you may be pleasantly surprised by the different perspectives which can be achieved by looking at things a little differently.

Most of all ... use all of your senses; experience and totally immerse yourself in the process. For, the rewards will be great.

It's All Timing

From those of you new to this process, the question often arises: When is the optimal time to go, for those dramatic fall colors?

In the case of the UP, one general answer suffices: from the very end of September through the first week of October. Another, perhaps more poetic, way of saying this would be: "When September turns to October, nature paints wonderful colors on its own, great canvas."

Traditionally, for most "normal years", this has been a good formula. You could venture up and almost time the different counties in this way, roughly following each for a few days, as colors changed. Plus, areas further inward - away from Lake Superior - tend to turn first; while those close by the shoreline turn more into October. This is due to the warming effect of water. Granted, "Gitche Gume", as the late Gordon Lightfoot immortalized, it is quite cool or cold; but at many times, even it is warmer than the surrounding air.

This is true with a normal September; cool, sunny days, and some cold overnights - with even some frosts thrown in.

But in recent years, with increased warming, the color lagging has been extended. In fact, some recent Septembers have been quite warm with no frosts occurring overnight at all.

Perhaps this is due to global warming, perhaps not; and this is not to say which side of that larger issue I fall on, but only to say that, in general, for accelerated fall colors, what I have noticed is that cooler/colder stretches do speed things up some. Plus, I have also noticed that the amount of rain, or dryness in the summertime, does have some effect; but have not found that to be very dominant. Although, I have also noticed that too much dryness or rain can leave a few trees in an unhealthy state as well.

It is also interesting to note that regardless of weather patterns of the summertime preceding it, there is one aspect of nature that is almost exactly the same every year no matter what. That is the angle of the sun, which is the same every September 15th, 20th; October 1st, etc.

There are also many good online articles on the causes of autumn color, but for our purposes here, suffice it to say that it is actually the result of a complex formula which includes things like reduced daylight, amount of rain, sunshine, etc. Not only this, but from year to year, one will notice that a different area will put on colors of slightly varying intensity; never quite the same.

It is also interesting to note that the yellows in many leaves are, to some extent, "already there" due to the retention of carotenoid pigments (xanthophylls). In other words, when the chlorophyll level drops, that particular color becomes prominent. However, the process of reds developing with the chemical anthocyanins and sugars is different.

Of course, it is a coincidental, beautiful fact that much of this occurs at the same time, so that often, many colors come into display at once as the trees prepare for winter. You also find that maples kick in a bit before the aspens and larch; but even so, there is still a beautiful overlap.

For now, though, suffice it to say that one primary cause is also reduced daylight and its effects on reduced chlorophyll. So, every year on the same date, the angle of the sun is pretty much the same as every other year. This much is a constant.

Ultimately, this almost "forces" the trees to be reminded to change color.

In certain years, you might get some colors which are weak, or muted, but in others, glorious, intense ones crop up. Obviously, the latter is the preferred scenario, but one can never tell.

In my world, this is one thing, along with the prior-mentioned yearly variance (even on the same trees), that is part of the "fun of the chase." It wouldn't be quite as fun if we could rigidly predict with certitude the exact date every year that a given area would produce the exact types of colors.

The fun of it involves that level of uncertainty, which will only be resolved by one going to certain spots to get a close look. Although with modern technology, like the omnipresent webcams, one can simply go online and see the progress of the changing colors, but for more fun, I would refrain from this. In fact, I would simply say that if you look online, check for areas which are either approaching or at peak. Then ... head up there.

Also, up in the UP, I have found certain areas to be quite "time sensitive." Even if colors are lagging, it might take only several days for them to-all of a sudden-gloriously burst forward only for the leaves to drop a few days after this. So, keep this in mind during your planning as well.

One prominent example, in my experience, is the stretch of hardwoods along US Highway 41 in Baraga County. The end of September is a good general rule; but if lagging occurs, then the first few days in October will work. But beware: Those leaves drop pretty quickly after peak.

As a final example, in 2020, the normal formula worked very well. I noticed that a couple of times, even by mid-September, overnight temperatures even dropped down to the upper 20s! So, I knew that the normal formula would hold.

We went up there and ... voila! Colors were a bit ahead, in great shape, with rich saturation dominating. The reds were really popping also.

In general, another pleasing fact about the UP is the colors tend to be pretty consistent from year to year, compared to a few other areas of the country. If you take in several counties, you are going to be amazed by a good portion of large areas, rarely with poor color display.

More on Timing

In a very-good year, one might head up first to Baraga County around September 28th; then northwest to Ontonagan County into early October and end up heading all the way east to the Munising area where colors generally peak a bit later (October 5th or so being a good general bet for the latter). Areas right along Lake Superior lag even later, going further into October.

So, it's always important to follow weather patterns in September, which I have often termed the "trigger month" as in the above example. Then, you will be in a better position to make your decisions in terms of both colors, and lodging. For those of you who might want to camp out, you might be in a better position still- as you can time your own accommodations pretty much the way you want.

Thankfully, one of the best ways you can do this in the modern age is via online sites. A couple of my favorites are: funintheup.com, and uptravel.com. For the latter, starting about September 20th, there is a section that gives rough percentages of color changes currently going on and those in terms of prediction for the weeks just ahead.

On funintheup.com, Steve Jurmu does a great job of actually giving weekly updates, even starting in August! The physical work he puts in on the road is a lot to be praised.

His general rule for timing is also a good one: If you come up in the last 4 days of September to the first 4 days of October, you should be in good shape.

These valuable resources will help your planning even more.

Weather, Daylight Hours, and Cautions on Driving

As I mentioned earlier, early fall often brings with it some of the best weather of the year and the UP is no exception.

However, as a caution, with the onset of October, it can get cold up there, even with light snow on occasion (which happened to us in 2020, early October, on the drive up to Keweenaw. Then, in the long UP winter ... numerous, groomed snowmobile trails dot the counties, giving many who enjoy that, lots of opportunities as well). So, you have to be prepared for this possibility, and bring along the appropriate clothing. I also recommend rain gear and good, sturdy hiking boots, of course.

But in general, if you are doing at least a week up there at this time, you will also get some splendid days: sunshine, mid 60s, calm, and blessed with those classic colors of the hardwoods, including larch (which turn a bit later in October, before dropping their needles.)

Another reality is the reduced hours of daylight at this time of year. Unlike the longer summer days, you are now working with shorter ones; so, it's best to rise early, and take full advantage of daylight while trying to minimize time on the road in the dark as well.

Dangers also increase with this. If you do end up driving in the dark, be especially careful of the numerous deer which are often out at dusk this time of year.

This is particularly true of those roads which are two lanes and have rows and rows of trees which hug the side of the road. Prominent cases that come to mind are the federal forest highways like 16 and 13. Just be very cautious when traveling these, pull off very carefully, be aware of logging trucks. Try to avoid such roads at night, if at all possible.

Also, when going down some roads, the visual feast will be plentiful and you may just find yourself wanting to stop your vehicle many times, as I have done over the years. US Highway 41, as it works its way across the peninsula, is a prime example.

Just use common sense when doing so, find sensible spots to pull well off, and use your ears to listen for traffic in both directions. Make your trip as safe as possible!

Film Techniques

I almost can't believe how I now talk about "the old days" of film; but for those of us old enough to remember the glory days of using it, much of the process was quite an experience. For me, there was a different kind of excitement implicit in the process as I would load rolls of Agfa print or Velvia slides into my Nikon. Another level of anticipation would result as I kept thinking, "I can't wait to see what this shot is going to look like when I get it developed."

In fact, one of my pleasures was also being able to present the imagery to my folks who were, at the times, well past being able to physically go to many hiking spots anymore. So, in a sense, they kind of vicariously lived part of the experiences through my eyes and mind. But later, with the dominance of digital technology, I simply did the same via TV; and now, computer screens and smart phones.

Their reaction to most of it, well, as that classic commercial would say ... "Priceless".

But nowadays, it's a different world, for better or worse. With instant gratification/results being desired by so many, folks simply prefer to use their phones, as some android and iPhones do produce remarkable imagery; while some of us still use our trusted DSLRs or, a combination of both.

To this day in fact, I still use both my 2006, Sony @ 100 (now somewhat obsolete), and recent Androids like my Hauwei and now the Galaxy a53 (the latter, mostly for videos; though, of course, I could upgrade to a

Sony camera which does both - stills and video; however, for the time being, I'm still fine.)

To get the most out of the UP, though, I still recommend a good DSLR with tripod; in particular, not only to capture different aspects of those waterfalls in motion, but to capture general imagery at its highest level. Since the UP is loaded with these, you want to maximize your results. Plus, some good basic lenses, and filters like the indispensable circular polarizer, and grad-neutral filter. This will give your work a more complete feel. For those of you taking it into the "Adobe Lab", another level can still be added.

You might also want to take an occasional black and white image or even adapt that special infrared filter for dramatic effect. Just remember that it's important to consciously remind yourself to do this. Many a time, I simply forget to do so as I generally get so overwhelmed with color, that it's hard to think about shooting any other way. I also realize that with many modern devices, one can simply add some of these effects later on.

Generally, a good DSLR in the Nikon, Canon, or Sony category - even 8 or 10 MP, will give you quality results. In fact, for years now with my 10.2 MP Sony, I have made quality enlargements up to 12 by 18 inches, and canvas prints up to 16 by 24 inches - both with excellent sharpness and color saturation still intact. Though I will admit, many cameras nowadays are at MP ranges of 16, 18, or well into the 20s- giving you excellent image quality as well.

One additional thing I would say about waterfall shooting: It's generally best on overcast days, to avoid harsh contrast. Though, there is little we can do about what Mother Nature provides. However, on occasion, you can still get some very nice images of them in full sunlight and add those surrounding colors (see the Power House waterfall shot in Baraga County on page 40 as an example.)

And for those of you maximizing on your phones, the numerous waterfalls will give you exciting opportunities to utilize crisp videos as well. Much like with stills, just use a steady hand or tripod if possible and try to capture the falls from different angles. One of my very-favorite examples is shooting autumn leaves in streams, with the given waterfall or cascades in the background.

It's also worth noting that many phones now do have tripod capability as well. So, if the phone is your choice, I would say to invest in a good tripod, and you'll be set.

Just take your time and enjoy the process. As one ace camera technician once told me years ago, when it comes to your choice of camera, "Two things come to mind. One, how comfortable you are with using it and two, how good the results are."

The Heart of the Action

With these tempting appetizers given, we now get closer to the main course. I therefore now begin with what I term a "simulated trip". This means that, we will assume that normal September with lots of sunshine, sunny days, and cool nights. Granted, this simulation for me over the years has been a reality and I have done things in the exact order I am presenting them to you here, including our 2020 trip (Jill and I). So, this could be very real for you as well.

I will admit that at times, on a more-constrained budget, I have also taken another exciting slice of what I term a "truncated", or shortened, trip. In this instance, I would focus on one county, perhaps part of a second and hope to hit the jackpot with colors. This happened most recently on my 2022 trip.

If you decide to do this, the MINUMUM I would recommend is 3 or 4 overnights. Even this is kind of a stuff job, but if you time things just right, you will still be rewarded with dazzling colors. If necessary, you can also take a day trip to another area which does have peak colors going on. I will shortly describe a trip when coming up from the south, Illinois through Wisconsin; but for those of you coming from different areas of the country, just use the information on timing in the different sections.

You can also utilize this book as a general travel guide to pick out specific areas to explore. This will be best for those of you passing through in limited time.

I will also add that what follows in terms of a trip sketch is meant as a solid guide, not an absolute. Although it can actually be utilized in the manner I present, you may find situations in which you can't possibly accomplish what I list for each day. Hopefully though, because you are blown away by some areas and want to put more time into one or two.

This is understandable. So, I would recommend that from the readings, you select some that you believe will really "hit the spot" for you. Don't try to rush things or jam them into some predetermined schedule. Take your time, and perhaps sacrifice a couple of stops.

It's OK; because hopefully, I will lay the groundwork for return trips to the UP and in subsequent books, I hope to expand upon some of these with additional information updated as I explore more. This just may apply to ones I might also do on those other fall "hot-spot" areas I mentioned earlier.

Roadside Parks and Recreation Passes

I just want to add a brief word about Michigan's fine roadside parks.

These were actually started by Herbert F. Larsen of the UP. One park along US Route 2 is named in his honor and I will mention it later on. These are peaceful, scenic areas right off the main highway that have facilities, picnic benches, and pleasant scenery to explore for folks of all ages. They differ somewhat from rest areas, which one finds along our interstates, but the idea is kind of the same.

A great quote of his, referring to their ideal usage: "living forest memorial of virgin hardwoods so that posterity could see and enjoy what nature had richly bestowed upon us."

As we go along, I will mention some special ones. For an exhaustive listing, refer to the Michigan Department of Transportation's website (michigan.gov/mdot).

Also, for current rates on Michigan's numerous state parks, it is best to check websites like https://www.michigan.gov/dnr/places/state-parks, to get the updated rates. Unfortunately, this, like most things, is one that increases over the years.

Maps

Here is a basic one. It can also be found on https://www.uptravel.com/, or other online resources. Also, it is probably a good idea to have some topographic maps so that you can see more detailed breakdowns of certain areas.

Plus, nowadays on our phones, we can simply utilize a resource like Google Maps as well. In general, though, with what I will present going forward, you won't actually need much more than what is here.

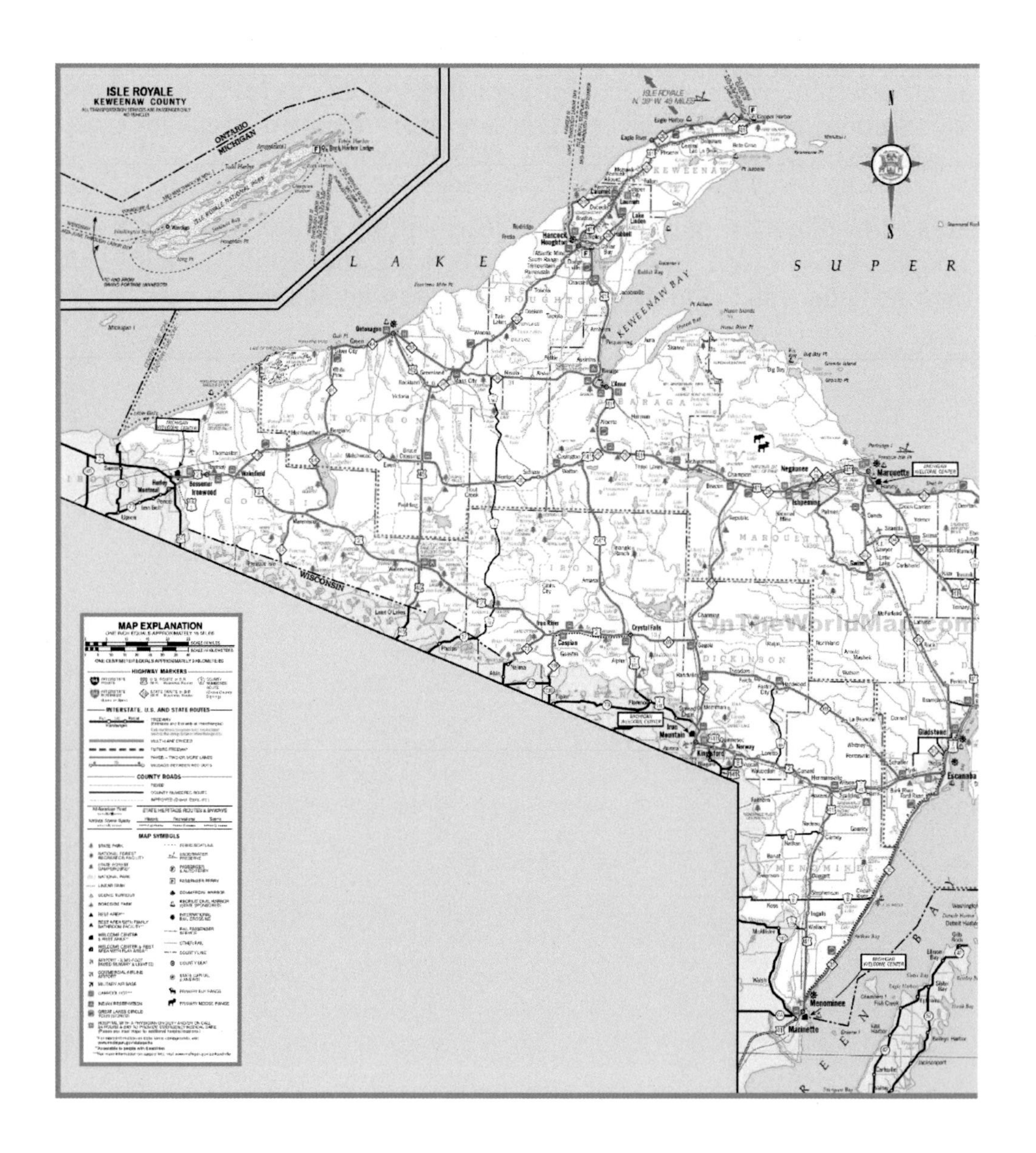
ISLE ROYALE
KEWEENAW COUNTY
ONTARIO
MICHIGAN
N
S
L A K E
S U P E R
KEWEENAW BAY
WISCONSIN
Hancock
Houghton
Ontonagon
L'Anse
Wakefield
Bessemer
Ironwood
Negaunee
Ishpeming
Marquette
Iron River
Caspian
Crystal Falls
Iron Mountain
Kingsford
Norway
Gladstone
Escanaba
Menominee
Marinette
MAP EXPLANATION
HIGHWAY MARKERS
INTERSTATE, U.S. AND STATE ROUTES
COUNTY ROADS
MAP SYMBOLS

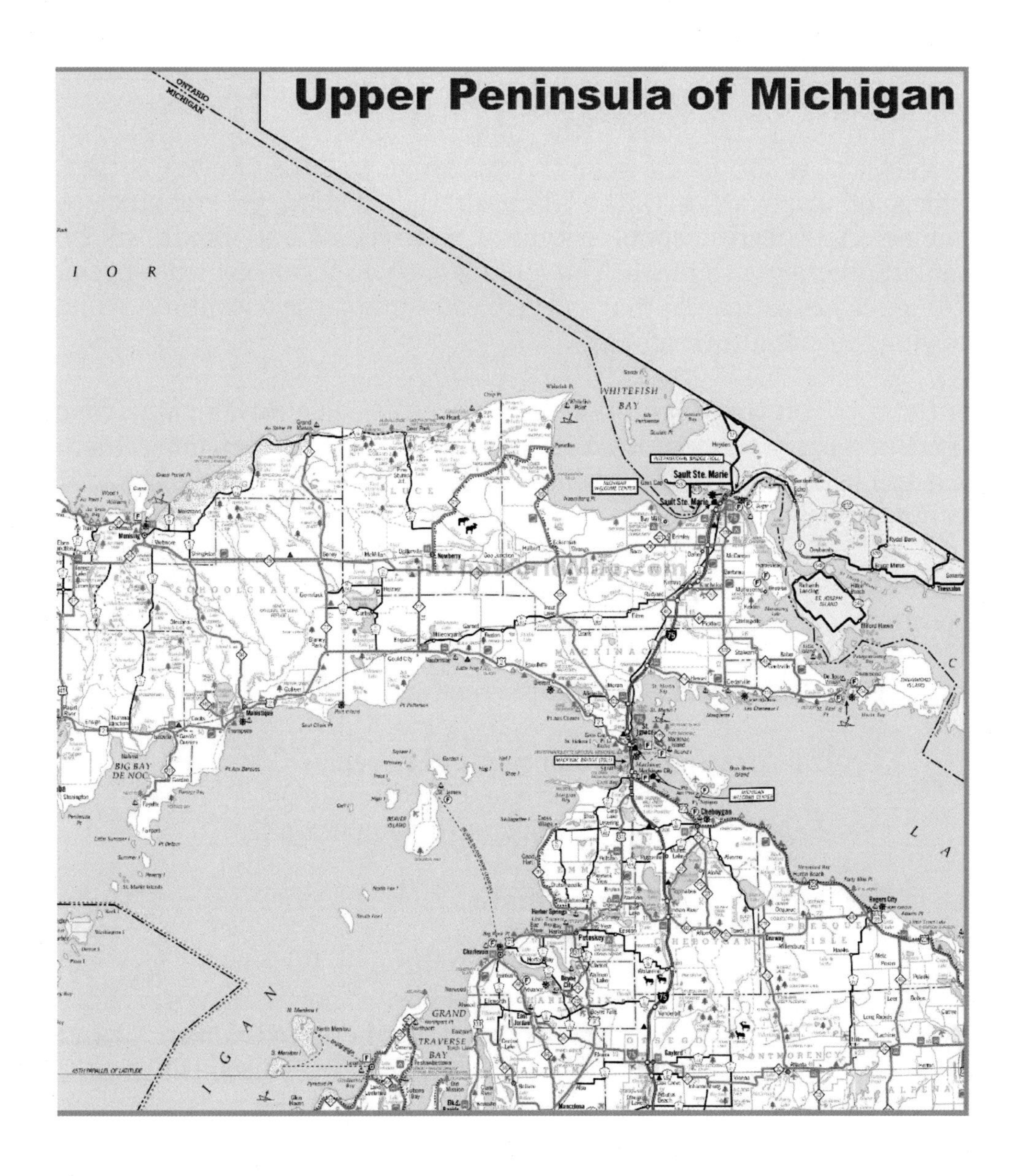

Upper Peninsula of Michigan
ONTARIO
MICHIGAN
WHITEFISH BAY
Sault Ste. Marie
BIG BAY DE NOC
GRAND TRAVERSE BAY

The Counties

Where to go first?

What follows in this book - the material about places, times, and experiences - is not meant to be an exhaustive analysis of every corner, scenic spot, or attraction of the UP, but rather, a solid, general guide to some selected, terrific spots – kind of a survey course. Some will be popular, others not so much. Though, I will try to focus on some special off-the-beaten-path areas that will give you some sense of solitude, while enjoying the magnitude of it all.

For those of you with high interest in places like Isle Royale, Mackinac Island, or parts of the counties that you want to explore even more, there are a number of good online resources. (Refer to the back of the book for a comprehensive list). I will occasionally mention some favorite places to eat and lodge, plus areas of unique attraction. As the years pass, some of these will change or the proprietors will move on, but hopefully, the important constant will be: the great scenic areas.

The book is roughly broken into three sections:

Central (Iron/Baraga/Marquette/Keweenaw Counties)
West (Ontonagon/Gogebic Counties)
East (Alger/Schoolcraft/Luce/Delta Counties)

The Colors of Northern Wisconsin

If you are traveling up from the south through Wisconsin, you will definitely want to take little hikes into some of northern Wisconsin's better spots: Dave's Falls [Old 141 Road, Amberg, Wisconsin 54102; 16TDR2274538545] or Long Slide Falls [Niagara, Wisconsin 54151; 16TDR2733959297].

Long Slide County Park and Falls is more isolated, not as crowded as Dave's Falls but it will provide you with mixed colors, pines, and a powerful waterfall experience that you won't soon forget. The road that goes into the Long Slide area, come the end of September to the beginning of October, is rich with maples and will be a good primer for many colors to come. They are a sort of "yardstick" as well. If the leaves are vibrant at the very end of September, you should be in good shape for what's to follow in terms of timing. But if these are turning a few days later, then much of the UP will also. This is not an absolute rule, by any means, but it is meant as a general-trend indicator.

To reach the area, keep heading far north of Green Bay on US Highway 8/141, past the tiny town of Pembine. You will have to cross a couple of branches of the Pemebonwon River. Head north, pass Heller Lane, on the right. Watch for the sign to Long Slide County Park on the right via Morgan Park Road [16TDR2597561458]. You will want to take this in about a mile to the Long Slide Falls Trailhead [Long Slide Road, Niagara, Wisconsin 54151; 16TDR2738959341].

The power of Long Slide Falls after hiking to the bottom of the canyon.

The canyon going down to the base of the falls is now paved to make it easier. Though, I must admit, in prior years, I enjoyed working through the rich vegetation more; it also added a nice color palette to the surroundings, some of which is still intact.

You can also work the top of the river and the small cascades in it. This is only a short distance from the parking area (which as of this writing was still a reasonable $3 per day, per vehicle.)

Smalley Falls [20545 Morgan Park Road, Niagara, Wisconsin 54141; marinettecounty.com; 16TDR2644260799] - About a half a mile north upstream, you can also visit the more compact area of Smalley Falls. It is also rewarding and less traveled; there is a small road sign where you make a short detour into a gravel parking area.

Return to US Highway 141, and head north. Depending on your timing, you can go east, briefly, on US Highway 8 toward Piers Gorge and the UP border or go west to enjoy the colors of Wisconsin's Florence County toward the UP and into Iron County. Since Piers Gorge typically peaks around October 4th or later, it is best to save that for the end of your trip.

What's fun about heading into far northern Wisconsin is that the colors start to pick up quite a bit. In some areas you see rows and rows of colors really popping.

Niagara, Wisconsin and the Menominee River

As you head up US Highway 141 toward the UP border, you will briefly pass through the tiny town of Niagara, Wisconsin just before the UP border. You will definitely want to check out the hardwoods and reflections along the dividing line, the Menominee River.

Often, the birch trees and mixed colors will be almost glass still in the scene- giving you nice reflections.

Reflections on the Menominee River, early October 2022

This is a good introduction to the UP and will give you an exciting feel or appetizer for what is to come.

To reach our next spots, you cross into the UP and go through Iron Mountain, Michigan. This may be a good time for a bite to eat or drink, as there are many restaurants and accommodations here. Continue on US Route 2/Highway 141 back into Florence County, Wisconsin, then north into the UP again.

An alternate way of heading up to Baraga County is via M-95. Though, I will save this for the end of the book as it makes a nice alternative for coming back- with plenty of larch and aspens turning.

Florence, Wisconsin - If you have time, stop in the quaint little town of Florence, about 14 miles northwest of Iron Mountain, at the cute little spot - *Maxsells Suites and Celebrations* [209 Central Avenue, Florence, Wisconsin 54121; http://www.maxsellsrestaurant.com/; 16TDR0342386141] along Fisher Lake, with the *Ice-Cream Shoppe* [232 Central Avenue, Florence, Wisconson 54121; 16TDR0339186198] across the street. It is a nice, tasty little surrounding that will give you a pleasant break. If you time it just right, you will hear the classic church bells ring on the hour.

Horserace Rapids [Horserace Rapids Road, Crystal Falls, Michigan 49920; 16TDR0158393797] - Now back on US Highway 2/141, keep heading northwest and you are back in the UP as you cross the Brule River. Head north and take a right heading east off US Highway 2/141 on Iron County Airport Road [16TCR9837196548]. Continue for about 1.5 miles. At the fork [16TDR0083595688], hang right and stay on Horserace Rapids Road for about another 1.5 miles. Go slowly for this semi-rough road takes you around some interesting high country to the end of the road. Then down to the hike toward Horserace Rapids on the Paint River.

Occasionally, kayakers hit the rapids with vigor, which is definitely a fun and exciting possibility. However, one of the real treats of this area is the very first overlook of the canyon, not far from the parking area.

From this vantage point, you can see not only down to the Paint River and some of those rapids, but also get a sea of mixed colors below.

Overlook of the canyon at Horserace Rapids Nature Trail

This is a prime example of the mixed hardwoods all around. It's just a pleasant general area in which to experience fall.

After Horserace Rapids, continue traveling north along US Highway 2/141, through the peaceful little town of Crystal Falls, Michigan [16TCS9688705776]. Continue north on US Highway 141 for approximately 35 miles to the intersection M-28 [16TCS8216755919]. Continue east on M-28/US Highway 141 for approximately 4 miles to the intersection of US Highway 41 [16TCS8721260132]. Turn left and head north on US Highway 41, which is a historic highway in its own right. It actually starts way up in Keweenaw and runs all the way down to Miami, Florida. If you are driving this at night, be as careful as you can.

It's about 53 total miles from Crystal Falls to our overnight target: L'Anse, Michigan [16TCS8904479150].

Your first overnight target should be right in Baraga County along US Highway 41. Come the end of September in a good year, you will find colors here to be about as brilliant and saturated as anywhere in our entire country.

In general, over the years I have found the color punch in Baraga and Keweenaw counties to be the greatest.

For those doing the truncated trip, L'Anse is also a good baseline to use US Highway 41 to head up to Keweenaw, as it's closer than Ontonogan.

Along US Highway 41, there are some economical accommodations. One could stay a couple nights near the tiny town of L'Anse or further west in Baraga. *L'Anse Motel and Suites* [960 US Highway 41, L'Anse, Michigan 49946; https://lansemotel.wixsite.com/lansemotel; 16TCS9003078194] provides decent, economical accommodations and John has been a good host.

Right off US Highway 41 in L'Anse come this time of year; you will find good roadside produce stands. *Spiessl Produce*, which also has an outlet in Ishpeming, offers fruits, vegetables, and fruit juices from Fruitport Michigan that are delicious.

Day 2

Baraga County

Now, come morning, if you hit it just right, along US Highway 41 you will see rows and rows of stunning colors in Baraga County which rival that of any place in our country. In fact, much like the Keweenaw, you just might find that if you use your smart phone, just the act of scrolling through the wonderful pictures will produce a sort of sensory overload, a kaleidoscope of colors that will dazzle you and your audiences.

The colors along Beaufort Lake Road at the very end of September 2012

For a side trip, at the very end of September, the colors along Beaufort Lake Road [16TDS1077055236], which is right off of US Highway 41/M-28 approximately 28 miles from L'Anse towards Marquette and skirts along Beaufort and George Lake, perfectly illustrates the dramatic power of Baraga County hardwoods. Simply stunning to observe, especially up against those crisp-blue skies.

Power House Falls - Now back to our trip. If you head south down US Highway 41 from L'Anse, only about 1 mile, one of your first spots will be Power House Falls [L'Anse, Michigan 49946; 16TCS8967376966]. Watch for the sign off US Highway 41, to the right, which simply reads "Power Dam Road" [16TCS9087476933] (The sign may be faded; however, the *Reid Funeral Chapel* is on the southwest corner of the intersection.) You will want to take this west a short distance, around a curve, going south; then it turns into manageable dirt, crosses over railroad tracks, and turn north changing into Power House Road. Take Power House Road to the end of the road where you will come upon the power house, about a mile total distance. You will get nice hardwoods accompanying you and will generally find it to be quiet, with minimal crowds around.

Hardwoods along Power Dam Road

At the waterfall area you can work around the powerhouse and get general views from the side and top of this 15-footer, but I actually prefer near the top where you can get various hardwoods mixed in with the upper stream.

Hardwoods with the upper stream at Power House Falls.

Definitely work your way around upstream (just to the left of the area the previous picture). There is almost an entire other, little world of cascades to explore here and with few, if any, other visitors. You can even work several blocks in to experience multiple cascades and forest.

You can also reverse the order and comfortably visit this area when you return to your lodging later in the day.

Continuing to Tour US Highway 41

Return to US Highway 41 and continue heading south/southeast. You will start to notice amazing hardwood colors and little ponds for reflections. If you find a spot, mostly on the right going south, try and pull off safely to take advantage of the beautiful scenery.

If you are at the peak of the season, a must drive/area is that of Baraga Plains Road, several miles south on US Highway 41, out of L'Anse and just before the tiny town of Alberta.

Turn right off US Highway 41 [16TCS8692167391] and only blocks in the display of hardwoods here is sublime. There is a quarry area to the north. At or close to peak, you might find a powerful scene like this:

In this image, the colors are getting close to peak, but you can also see all the little shrubs below turning. So, you see subtle shades right before maximum impact.

If time permits, you can take a little detour to Ogemaw Falls, a little waterfall a mile and a half down Baraga Plains Road from US Highway 41, in a tiny area on the west side [16TCS8469166912]. You might find only one little area to park just down the road but be careful, it's tight. The countryside around it seems almost Western.

Here, you will definitely find another little gem where you probably will not encounter much competition.

Lake Plumbago, Alberta

The next main target, about 8 miles south of L'Anse and less than a mile from Baraga Plains Road, is the splendid spot of Plumbago Lake in Alberta. As you approach, you will pass the lake on your left/east side. Just past the lake is tiny Preacher Park [21235 Alberta Avenue #2, L'Anse, Michigan 49946; 16TCS8682866608]. A distinct marker is a large sign for the Michigan Technological University Ford Center on the

Lake Plumbago from Preacher Park

right, across US Highway 41 from the park. The park has a small sign and picnic bench by the water.

When you stop, be very careful of the fast traffic along US Highway 41 travelling in both directions. Make sure to pull into the small lot very rapidly and use your ears to listen for oncoming traffic.

As the photo hints, generally, come the very end of September or very-early October, this is another gem spot to enjoy and meditate by in the midst of splendid colors.

Canyon Falls Roadside Park and Canyon Falls

Just over a mile south of Preacher Park on US Highway 41, we come upon Canyon Falls Roadside Park [Old US Highway 41, L'Anse, Michigan 49946; 16TCS8738964792], an area that is not only one of my favorite places to hike in the UP- but in the entire country as well!

Canyon Falls Roadside Park, late September 2020

As previously mentioned, all across the UP, you will find roadside parks, and this one is an absolutely prime, special example.

The convenience of this spot is obvious. The signs for this classic roadside park are clear on the right (west) side heading south, with plenty of picnic benches and decent latrines. At peak time, the very end of September to the beginning of October, the maples in the lot will put on a special show of their own.

But that is only at the entrance. You will want to spend lots of time in this stunning educational spot so be prepared with maybe a backpack loaded with snacks, water, and camera gear.

Start your hike following the Canyon Falls Trail going downhill through rich mixed forest. My personal favorite time is actually right after rains have come - for not only do you have stronger flows in the river and cascades, but that unmistakable aroma of autumn as you hike. It's just glorious.

Keep going, and you will discover that the sounds of US Highway 41 magically fade away, eventually giving way to soothing sounds of the Sturgeon River and its tributaries.

Beautiful hardwoods along the Canyon Falls Trail

On the way down, you will pass through a fern swamp with good boardwalks over tiny cascades. This alone would already justify stopping here. Although I prefer this area on an overcast day, if you hit it just right, look skyward too on sunny days- for you just might catch a stunning display of hardwoods.

I can't stress enough how powerful the autumn experience is here; the park is simply jam packed with all you need: sky, colors, water, cascades, boardwalk, tiny bridges, and variation in landscapes that will not only refresh, but educate you as well.

Keep hiking along the river for different perspectives of smaller waterfalls ringed by colors. Further along be sure to check out one of the rare red pine, with an obvious sign attached to it, explaining the genealogy.

Another beautiful shot from further downstream

If you keep going, approximately a half a mile, you will get to the main, powerful waterfall where there are wooden fences at the Canyon Falls Lookout [16TCS8692064285].

Be very careful in this area of the canyon, especially after it rains, as the surfaces can get quite slippery. The Sturgeon River is no joke. It is powerful, so give it the respect it deserves, but it truly exemplifies the power of water.

Self-portrait in front of the main Canyon Falls waterfall drop from 2015.

Past the main waterfall, you can hike up the ridge just south to get a grand view of the canyon; sometimes referred to as “The Grand Canyon of the UP”. Then hike along the top, going all the way around, for different views of the river down below all complemented by rich, changing, complex forests. There are at times, even a rope or two down in part of it, presumably for those summer adventurers who dare to take in the river. At times, divers jump off the cliffs into the river!

If you venture this way in the summer months and are daring enough, go for it. However, in the early autumn, temperatures will generally be too cold, in both air and water, to permit this.

Follow the trail as far back as you like, in the form of a large “U” before you return to the parking lot. By all means, spend some quality time here. If you spend hours here on a pleasant day, you will instantly feel the rewards.

It’s also pet friendly. On occasion, I recall touching moments when some hikers have had their blind dogs in as well.

It’s a classic example of the best of autumn.

Continuing South along US Highway 41

Upon exit, you will want to head south and then east to keep exploring the fall treasures along US Highway 41.

Alongside the highway, you might even find a gem like this.

This is another strong image which shows complex colors occurring from the smallest bushes to the tallest trees, with pines thrown in for good measure.

You may want to stop along US Highway 41 to take some similar photographs. If so, just remember to remain cautious and as careful as you can with the fast traffic along the highway.

As you head east, a different topography unfolds. You may even get early glimpses of the larch in the swamplands around the highway as they begin to turn.

Be sure to stop along Lake Michigamme - a nice, large lake. Come this time of year, it is ringed with stunning color displays, even at the Roadside Park on the west end of the lake, just past the small community by the same name. That powerful image along Beaufort Lake Road on Page 38 comes from this area.

The McCormick Wilderness

For our next main target, we will sneak into the western part of Marquette County. The trees here generally turn at the end of September; although, if timing is lagging, then October 3rd through 5th can be a good bet as well.

Therefore, you will want to accomplish this now; for, when you return only a few days later, there is a good chance that the colors will be past their peak and the leaves will have dropped. So, we want to take advantage now at the end of September.

Let's briefly step into my "Way-Back Machine" again, to 2002. I remember reading about this area in one of my rare, good hiking books on Michigan, aptly titled, *Hiking Michigan* (by Roger E. Storm and Susan M. Wedzel, 1997 edition; but updated in 2009). At the time, it was the only source I knew of which discussed this isolated area.

As I drove along the road, I was stunned at the complexity of forms and colors present. It was another of those revelations. Plus, as previously hinted at, this is an area which has features that seem like they are out of the Desert Southwest.

To get there, you will want to head east of Lake Michigamme and be prepared to turn left (north) on County Road 607/Huron Bay Grde [16TDS2283453577]. Just past the *Our Redeemer Lutheran Church* it's located, on the left-hand (north) side of US Highway 41 and the Michigamme Shores Campground on the right-hand (south) of US Highway 41. Be careful as this is another spot which can come up quickly. If you cross the Peshekee River, you have gone too far.

You will want to take this road for several miles into the area as it parallels and crosses the Peshekee River. Even though the road is paved, it still needs to be improved. The roller-coaster effect can really get to be a bit much. (Update: As of 2019, the first few miles in are nicely paved and smoother.)

This is an excellent area for photographing different types of hardwoods and getting some prime "down-a-fall-road" shots.

Here once again you have a prime combination of water, mixed hardwoods, and sky that exemplifies autumn in the UP.

The serenity of the area along County Road 607 looking east across the Peshekee River.

If you choose to go all the way, Arfelin Lake [16TDS1882464481], which boasts similar scenic beauty, turn left (west) onto South Arfelin Lake Road [16TDS2029864850]. Be prepared because this is a narrow side road and is a bit tight.

Back to L'Anse or Baraga

Now, time to double back, all the way north/northwest on US Highway 41 and into either L'Anse or Baraga, depending on where you are spending the night.

This has been a long day, but if time permits, I definitely recommend the next two spots northeast of L'Anse. If not, then the next morning they can be done on Day 3. It all depends on how you feel at the end of a splendid day.

Pinery Indian Cemetery

For the Pinery Indian Cemetery, you want to pass through L'Anse. Take East Broad Street, right (east) of US Highway 41 at the Baraga County Convention and Visitor's Bureau (It has a huge "INFORMATION" sign on the roof) [16TCS8971678409], pass under the "Welcome to L'Anse – Village by the Bay" sign, and head northwest to Main Street (one block before Broad Street ends). Turn right and continue northeast. At Jentoft Road it turns into Skanee Road. Continue northeast to the second road to the right and turn right (east) onto Indian Cemetery Road [16TCS9044881628]. (The total mileage from downtown Broad Street to Indian Cemetery Road is approximately 1.75 miles.)

Continue east on Indian Cemetery Road for approximately 2.5 miles. The road will bend to the right (southeast) about 2/3 of the way to the Pinery Indian Cemetery [Indian Cemetery Road, L'Anse, Michigan 49946; 16TCS9427180772]. Pull off and park on the circular drive through the cemetery and traverse the grounds peacefully.

Scene at the Pinery Indian Cemetery

This cemetery has been utilized by Native Americans since the 1600s (some American war veterans are also buried here) and the dominant

forms here are quaint little houses known as "Spirit Houses"- meant to help those passing on take things with them to the afterlife.
This is a peaceful and reflective setting that definitely possesses a uniqueness that you don't find in most cemeteries. Here as well, you are likely to find needed and appropriate solitude.

Silver Falls

Silver Falls is definitely another of those waterfall winners. A place you can peacefully explore, generally without the attendant crowds. So, you will want to put some quality time in.

Along its entire length, the Silver River has many powerful drops. Years ago, I was invited to explore and photograph some hidden parts of the river by some nice, local residents on their property. Although the drops discussed here are not the largest, they are fairly easy to reach.

To get to the falls, continue northeast on Skanee Road just over 5 miles, and watch for the Silver Falls Road sign on right (south) side of the road which comes up quickly [16TCS9796783940]; it also has a MI DNR post close to it, so it should be easily discernible.

Turn right (south) and take this road about half a mile down through mixed hardwoods and watch for the forks in the road. You will want to stay to the left for the small parking area, with its distinctive boulders [16TCS9797682990].

From here, take the short path to the top of the ridge over the river and get different vantage points of the river and rapids. You can work your way down to the top of the rapids and to the top of the falls themselves. View the power of the main drop as it blasts through a tight, narrow canyon. This is a prime opportunity for video work.

Keep following the trail below and you'll get other views.

Use caution here, especially after rainfall. The rocks out in the middle can get quite slippery.

Up close and personal with the Silver River from the top area.

A suggestive view is from the top with rich hardwoods adding to the splendor

In both of these spots, you can take some great videos too because the noise factor amplifies the feeling of overall power.

Don't forget to capture some scenes of the forest floor

The forest floor along the path

Big Eric's Bridge State Forest Campground and Big Erick's Falls

For those with extra time and an adventurous spirit, you may want to go even further along Skanee Road as it roughly follows the Silver River northeast and skirts along Huron Bay before turning east to its end point (approximately 12.5 miles from Silver Falls Road) where it forks off as either Portice to the left (north) or Erick Road to the right (southeast) [16TDS1551390889]. Follow Erick Road for approximately 1.25 miles, you will reach Big Eric's Bridge State Forest Campground [Skanee, Michigan; (906) 353-6558; 16TDS1739190684] and Big Erick's Falls on the East Branch of the Huron River.

Point Abbaye

To reach Point Abbaye [16TDT1349201611], take Skanee Road northeast for just over 2 miles. Turn left (north) on Townline

[16TDS0096985409]. Follow Townline north for approximately 4.5 miles. Turn right (east) onto Point Abbaye Road [16TDS0104292762]. Follow Point Abbaye Road for approximately 11 miles. If you decide to do this trip, be forewarned that the road turns to dirt and can get quite dusty. But if you feel your vehicle can handle it, go for it.

Ojibwa Casino

At the end of a long, rewarding day, you may choose to relax. For those of you with the penchant for it, the *Ojibwa Casino* (16449 Michigan Avenue, Baraga, Michigan 49908; 16TCS8488581849) is a fun spot.

A photograph with the faint crescent moon in the distance, just above the tree line that epitomizes the vast power of those UP hardwoods (at the intersection of M-38 and FH-16)

Day 3

Ontonagan County

As October gets close, you will want to head west to Ontonagan County for the second phase of your trip. The thrills coming up will be quite plentiful.

Bishop Baraga Shrine

We can start heading west on US Highway 41 and make a brief detour to the Bishop Baraga Shrine [17570 US Highway 41, L'Anse, Michigan 49946; 16TCS8749978309] which overlooks L'Anse Bay. The shrine is located just south of US Highway 41 off Boyer Road, approximately 1 mile west of L'Anse.

This is a neat spot and gives information about Bishop Frederic Baraga- who did important missionary work in the area, was skilled at Native American languages, and came to be known as 'The Snowshoe Priest" because he would travel hundreds of miles, with snowshoes, over many years of harsh winters. This is also a good spot for meditation, and information about the bishop.

Bishop Baraga Shrine

Baraga State Park

Once you leave the shrine, head northwest on US Highway 41 around the bay toward Baraga. If time permits, you might want to relax at Baraga State Park [1300 US Highway 41, Baraga, Michigan 49908; www.michigan.gov; (906) 353-6558; 16TCS8541379670] where you can get some interesting photographs close to railroad tracks. Continue north on US Highway 41 into Baraga. Turn left (west) onto M-38 (the stoplight) also known as Michigan Avenue and the Joseph H. Meagher Memorial Highway [16TCS8653681739]. Continue west out of Baraga, passing the *Ojibwa Casino* on your right (north)

Be prepared to stop for explosive hardwood colors!

Sturgeon River Gorge and Sturgeon Falls

For those of you who want to maximize your off-road travels, reduce crowds, and really dip deep into the Ottawa National Forest, I recommend the Sturgeon River Gorge and Sturgeon Falls. But hopefully in this case, you will have a rental vehicle, preferably a strong SUV. To get there, continue about 9.5 miles west of Baraga and turn left (south) off M-38 onto Prickett Dam Road [Also known as Silver Mountain Road; 16TCS7199780203].

At approximately 2.25 miles veer to the right on National Forest Development Road (NF)-2270 [16TCS7193576531]. From this point, it's about 9.8 miles in.

Try to have a good topographic map with you. The forks of forest roads here can get a bit confusing; so, you will want to have good maps and a working phone. Just try to stay on NF-2270 proper, after the turnoff from Prickett Dam Road as much as possible.

As you take NF-2270, deep back into the woods, color-changing hardwoods also unfold all around. You might want to take some photographs of these, but when you get to the Gorge area, you definitely will.

Find the marked parking area for the Sturgeon Falls Trailhead [NF-2270, Pelkie, Michigan 49958; Approximately 16TCS7111267290] and hike the steep canyon down to the falls. You will pass through beautiful mixed hardwoods, culminating with the power of Sturgeon Falls [Pelkie,

Michigan 49958; www.fs.usda.gov; (906) 932-1330; 16TCS7039666825].

Bear's Den Overlook

Back at the parking area, you can take a small detour south to Bear's Den Overlook. Continue on NF-2270 to the "T" intersection with Clear Creek [16TCS7180066645]. Turn right (southwest) and follow Clear Creek for approximately 0.1 miles. Here, you just might find an amazing view of a valley of mixed hardwoods, dominated by aspens. [16TCS7163666522]

View from Bear's Den Overlook

As a caution, be careful of flying insects. Even in early October, if the weather is warm, they can be quite an annoyance. Therefore, if they are present, minimize your time here, but still enjoy. It is one of those off-the-beaten-path areas that will be less crowded and highly rewarding.

Now, retrace your way back to M-38. Once you arrive at M-38, turn left and head west. There are the tiny communities of Laird and Nisula along this route which glow with color. At the intersection of M-38 and National Forest Road (NF) 16 [16TCS5445680811], approximately 11 miles from Prickett Dam Road, turn left (south).

National Forest Road 16 (NF-16)

You will now take a color-filled, 20-mile trip down NF-16 through the heart of the Ottawa National Forest. We break NF-16 into two segments: M-38 to M-28 and M-28 to US Route 2. The second segment ending at US Route 2 we will do as an alternate ending to another possible trip (Page 128).

Be cautious and exercise great care driving here, as this is a stretch of road where many trees hug the side of the road. The same caution should be exercised on the logging roads which intersect NF-16 at various spots.

The mixed hardwoods and complex scenes of this stretch all the way down to M-28 provide an abundance of thrills, including the side road to my namesake, Bob Lake.

The photograph below remains a personal favorite of my own work because of all the complex, mixed colors it exemplifies including the prominent maple on right with those deep, blood-red colors.

Photograph of the amazing colors along NF-16 approaching M-28

Kenton Cemetery

Moving along, about 4 miles north of Kenton, is Sparrow Rapids (worth a brief look; [Kenton, Michigan 49967; 16TCS5043851999]); then, just before the intersection of NF-16 with M-28, you will find the Kenton Cemetery on the right (west) [NF-16, Trout Creek, Michigan 49967; 16TCS5516750611]. Try and stop here for a nice excursion, with potent color punch. Walk the grounds; though, be prepared for some high emotion, as a couple of the graves indicate small children who passed away in the mid-1800s, even after living for only a few months.

The maples at their glorious peak at the Kenton Cemetery

Jumbo River Railroad Bridge

At the T-intersection with M-28 [16TCS5502949774], turn right (west). As you cross the Jumbo River (approximately 1.6 miles from the intersection with NF-16) [16TCS5237049951] look to your right (north) to see the Jumbo River Railroad Bridge [16TCS5236949988].

Golden Glow Road

If time permits, make an excursion down Golden Glow Road, the first road to the left (south) off of M-28 after the Jumbo River

[16TCS5193249946]. You will want to take Golden Glow Road south for a couple of miles. It is paved initially but turns into a dirt road that is still manageable for most cars.

There are good views of farmlands on the right (west) and trees on the left (east).

Approximately 1.6 miles south on Golden Glow Road you will come to a crossroad [16TCS5187147317]. At this point, continuing south the road becomes Forest Service Road (Ff) 4580. Golden Glow Road continues to the right (west) and Jumbo Pitt Road goes to the left (east).

Continue south on Ff4580 until it turns into trees all around. If the timing is right, you might capture some terrific, intimate "down-a-fall-road" photographs.

"Down-a-fall-road" photograph taken on Ff4580

When you can find a safe place to turn around, head back north on Ff4580.

If you are a bit more daring, as you head back north, you might want to take the detour on Jumbo Pitt Road [16TCS5187147317] east to the quarry where you will find the pleasant Jumbo Creek area.

At times along this, your vehicle might just barely clear the vegetation; so, I am not highly recommending it. But if you really want another good experience that is likely to be without the crowds, then go for it.

Jumbo Creek and Falls

Follow Jumbo Pitt Road (aka Golden Glow Road N) east to the fork in the road [16TCS5236547300]. Take the right fork (CR-4589-B) southeast to the old sand-quarry area. Park to the left (east) of the quarry [16TCS5315946378] and make your way to the Jumbo River.

Nice hardwoods are all around, as well as a nice bridge over the river that will give you different perspectives. It is an area with character all its own.

To reach Jumbo Falls, continue through the quarry and park by the brown trout sign [16TCS5303446083] and follow the foot path upstream to the falls [16TCS5305945870].

Agate Falls Scenic Site

Keep heading west on M-28 for approximately 7.75 miles from Golden Glow Road to the splendid Agate Falls Scenic Site on the left (south) side

Colors at Agate Falls at their peak intensity

of M-28 [16TCS3970649311]. Agate is approximately 9.5 miles west of Kenton.

Take the left into the main parking area, which in early October features a strong display of maples you won't soon forget.

Use the walking trail that passes underneath M-28 and go into the lot on the right, where a nice village gift-and-ice cream shop once stood.

Proceed back to the trail and viewing platform.

This is a powerful waterfall with a variety of possibilities. One option is hiking further down the steep and dangerous canyon to the base below, with views up to the M-28 bridge. If you are fairly fit and up to the task, then use extreme caution and hold on to roots and trees whenever possible. This is a demanding task, not to be taken lightly.

At the base, take your time to cherish the surroundings. Though much of the photography from this area will include M-28 above, as its bridge crosses the river.

For even further adventure, you can hike up above all of this and get some stunning views of the river all the way below in both directions. There is an old railroad grade which passes through that leads to the Agate Falls Railroad Bridge [16TCS3956849564]. You might see an occasional vehicle still come through. I give Jill credit for this find during our 2020 trip.

Back at the parking lot you might want to take advantage of the picnic area and perhaps explore the forest and river below here as well. It can have some surprising power in its own right. At peak time, the display of maples here tends to be quite stunning.

View of Agate Falls from the top

Bond Falls

Exit the parking lot from Agate Falls Scenic Site turning right (east) onto M-28 and double back approximately 2.75 miles to Mile W Road [16TCS4393749140]. Turn right (south) and follow the road. Along the way, if your timing is right, you will also find spots of tremendous colors to photograph, especially as you get closer to Bond. So, do this carefully and enjoy.

An example of the power of the mixed hardwoods with some subtle shades of pink thrown in for good measure from early October 2018

Just under a mile south, Calderwood Road will verge to the right (west) [16TCS4389747719]. Follow it to the right for approximately 5.5 miles as it winds its way through the Ottawa National Forest. As you approach Bond Falls Flowage, Calderwood Road will continue straight to the south, but you will want to take the right fork onto Bond Falls Road [16TCS3974441701] and follow Bond Falls Road for just over another 2 miles.

Just after you cross the bridge over the Middle Branch of the Ontonagon River (with the dam to your left) you will enter a tiny "village" here with gift shop (*Bond Falls Outpost*, 12371 Bond Falls Road, Bruce Crossing, Michigan 49912; 16TCS3628841613), picnic tables, and facilities. Stop here and enjoy ice cream if your palette is in the mood and the timing is right.

Just up to the right you will come across the scenic site of another UP classic: Bond Falls.

To get to the Bond Falls Loop Trailhead, follow Bond Falls Road to Scenic Overlook Drive, the first road to the right (north) [16TCS3602141529]. Follow the drive to the parking area for Bond Falls Loop Trailhead [Bruce Crossing, Michigan 49912; 16TCS3591941786]. The trailhead will be in the northeast corner of the parking lot.

This is still one of those spots which is, even when crowded, just a joy to visit: peaceful, classic waterfall views, and vigorous hikes around the falls You really can't go wrong here.

A splendid capture of the autumn scene from the base of Bond Falls

From the top of the stream, you will want to hike out a bit and work some shots in of the colored hardwoods above. You may even get a bonus reflection in the water at times.

As you work down the side of the falls, it is a good time for video work as well. Just be careful to watch your lenses afterward, as some condensation may form from the mist, especially if you are shooting from the side of the falls on the steps leading below.

Many years ago, there was a classic, old-fashioned bridge at the base but this was replaced a few years back by a more-modern one. As this is not as scenic as the prior bridge, you will want to get more shots of the falls themselves. It is recommended to hike around, and up to the other side as well.

In general, Bond Falls could be considered an "American Classic." It is a great spot to hike and enjoy nature. So, even if crowded, by all mean take in as much of it as you can.

O Kun-de-Kun Falls

For the next leg of this journey, we will exit the Bond Falls area via Bond Falls Road by taking it out the other way. Depart Scenic Overlook Drive and turn right (west) onto Bond Falls Road. Follow it for just over 3 miles as it winds through the forest, crossing Roselawn Creek, and paralleling the creek until it reaches US Highway 45 [16TCS3251240973]. Turn right (north) onto US Highway 45 and travel just over 9 miles to the intersection with M-28 at the little town of Bruce Crossing [16TCS3293555779]. Continue north on US Highway 45 for approximately 7.5 miles. After you cross the Baltimore River, watch for the green sign "N COUNTRY HIKING TRAIL / O KUN DE KUN FALLS," otherwise, you might miss it. Turn right (east) off the highway into the North Country Trail Parking and the O-Kun-De-Kun Falls Trailhead [16TCS3348268237].

As a precaution here, DO NOT take this trail if it has rained the same day or day before! The kind of mud back here is vicious and recently, I almost lost a good pair of shoes in the process.

The distance from the parking area to the falls will be about 1.3 miles and you will cross part of the North Country and All-Terrain Vehicle (ATV) trails. You will get a real education in hardwood types with their mixed colors.

Just off the main hiking trail is a spur to the Peanut Butter Falls [16TCS3509668524].

O Kun-de-kun Falls [16TCS3530568659] is a good one with a drop of over 20 feet. There is a suspension bridge [16TCS3539668677] downstream and it all makes for a nice, isolated, complete round-trip hike.

Ontonogan

Head back to US Highway 45 and turn right (north). You will continue to follow US Highway 45 through some hilly terrain and cross the Ontonagon River. At the "T" intersection [16TCS3592277470], US Highway 45 continues to the left (West) while M-26 goes to the right (east). Continue to follow US Highway 45 west and then north through Rockland (more on this later) to the coastal town of Ontonogan. One option for the night is *Scott's Superior Inn and Cabins* [Stroud Road, Ontonagon, Michigan; (906) 884-4866; www.scottssuperiorinn.com/; 16TCS2120192642].

Since 1992, Kathy and Don Scott have run a nice set of accommodations here with motels and cabins situated close to Lake Superior. Now, their son Josh and his wife Michelle are nicely carrying on the tradition. This can also be used as a baseline for day trips to the Porkies, Keweenaw, and beyond.

Day 4

Now that we are in early October, strong color possibilities keep unfolding. Today, we head west by southwest on M-64 west. M-64 turns to the south just prior to the Big Iron River and Silver City [16TCS0414589530]. Continue south on M-64 all the way south approximately 18 miles to M-28 and Bergland [16TCS0287963096]. On M-64 south, hardwood colors continue to burst forth and if you have extra time or an extra day, hikes into the Trap Hills will be a rewarding excursion. The views of aspen groves turning in particular will be another gem.

In Bergland, M-64 joins with M-28 as you continue to the west. The road skirts the pleasant shores of Lake Gogebic and takes you just over 20 miles to the town of Wakefield.

As you pass through Wakefield, if your timing is right and the air is still, you can get a marvelous reflection on Sunday Lake [16TBS7404251705]. Peaceful and tranquil is often the rule here.

In Wakefield, turn right (west) [16TBS7423251214] and continue on US Route 2 for approximately 5.5 miles to the town of Bessemer. Turn right (north) onto N Moore Street (The AD Johnson High School will be on the northwest corner of the intersection) [15TYM2624951732] and continue north for approximately 0.7 miles, where the road veers to the left (west) and becomes Black River Road [15TYM2620252913]. A half mile later, Black River Road will curve to the right (north) [15TYM2542352915] becoming County Road 513 and later the Black River National Forest Scenic Byway.

Take County Road 513 north approximately 16 miles until it ends at the Lake Superior shoreline at Black River Harbor [Ironwood, Michigan 49938; www.fs.usda.gov; 15TYM2590972122]. As this road is also a National Scenic Byway, come this time you will also be given a splendid color treat as you drive its length.

There are multiple waterfalls to hike through on the way as well. A couple of them involve some vigorous hikes, but are conveniently located adjacent to Country Road 513, right on the Black River.

Great Conglomerate Falls and Gorge Falls Trailhead

Great Conglomerate Falls [15TYM2543568504] is one example. Great Conglomerate Falls and Gorge Falls Trailhead is just off Black River Road [15TYM2464868525] As you pass through this forest, it almost seems tropical with large leaves below, and moisture all around. Just leave enough time to reach the Lake Superior shore.

For this, I will only sketch out a basic glimpse and save more discussion for its sister area: the Presque Isle River area of the Porkies, which I like even better.

Black River Harbor and Rainbow Falls

Once you have reached the northern most point of the Black River National Forest Scenic Byway, you will have arrived at Black-River Harbor [Ironwood, Michigan 49938; www.fs.usda.gov; 15TYM2590972122]. It is best to allow a decent amount of time to explore as you cross the bridge [15TYM2595872280] and head through a nice birch forest on the east side of the Black River; and then hike up to a great view of Rainbow Falls [15TYM2617771501].

View of Rainbow Falls

This is a powerful waterfall, with different vantage points. Mixed hardwoods will sprinkle the scene with greater splendor.

You might want to picnic back in the park area before heading all the way back down to Bessermer. If possible, try to do so before dark as Country Road 513 is one of those roads where the trees hug the sides of the road. Back in 2007, I experienced a deer collision at dusk, the prime time of their appearance. Needless to say, it was not a pleasant one.

Retrace your trip back to Ontonogan to spend the night. The trip from Black River Harbor to Ontonogan is approximately 72 miles and can take about 1.5 hours.

Day 5

As October moves along, we now take a long day trip up to the Keweenaw peninsula, one of my favorite UP areas of all. But on the way, more sites will continue to delight.

In fact, before we begin our journey today, I would say that the Keweenaw is one of those areas which is prime timber, so to speak, for those of you considering that truncated trip. Loaded with scenic and historical possibilities, it is the ideal area to devote days of exploring and enjoyment.

The basics of this journey are M-38 (Joseph H. Meagher Memorial Highway) southeast out of Ontonogan. Heading out on M-38, you will see lots of hardwoods alongside the road mixed in with nice farmlands.

Winona Lake

Just east of the small village of Greenland, M-38 will turn to the south [16TCS4366382692]. Continue straight (northeast) on M-26 through the twin cities of Hancock/Houghton (approximately 52 miles / 1 hour) In many normal years, many of the hardwood colors along M-26 turn at

Wonderful reflections of the trees on Winona Lake.

the end of September. However, if you are here in a year when you have some lag, then you will also experience a true winner; for the drive along M-26 at peak color is also stunning. Some prime examples are near the tiny town of Winona [16TCS5496291977] You might be lucky enough to catch splendid autumn reflections at Winona Lake, or as I term it, "Color" Lake [16TCS5451891736].

Marvelous colors that can be viewed from some of the side roads off M-26.

Twin Lakes State Park

Continue northeast to Twin Lakes State Park [6204 Poyhonen Road, Toivola, Michigan 49965 / (906) 288-3321; 16TCS5847694718] which boasts strong maples and the color festival along M-26 in general. It's truly amazing. At peak time, I highly rate the drive along M-26 as another stunner. The color-changing hardwoods that ring the road on either side provide quite a visual feast as they almost "compete" with one another for visual superiority.

You will pass through a number of small towns as you approach the twin cities of Hancock and Houghton. When you arrive in Houghton you will have multiple opportunities to pick up supplies, fuel, food, and more. Houghton is also home to Michigan Technological University.

Covered Drive

If you have some extra time, you might want to take the side detour to the Covered Drive (S-63 along Coles Creek Road) This is a classic drive through the canopy of trees, where you are underneath as they almost touch each other. To get there, turn left (west) onto P-554 (Houghton Canal Road)[16TCT7981919658] before reaching the Portage Canal Lift Bridge that crosses from Houghton into Hancock. Follow for approximately 2 miles and turn left (southwest) onto A-63 (Coles Creek Road [16TCT7679020687]. Follow Coles Creek Road (A-63 will change to S-63) westerly for approximately 3.7 miles. At the intersection with Larson Road [16TCT7099920705], continue straight (west) onto Covered Drive (S-63). Covered Drive continues for another 3.5 miles or so through the canopy of trees.

The Keweenaw Peninsula

The Keweenaw Peninsula is one of my favorite spots in the entire UP, and country as well. A 50-mile stretch of land that juts out into Lake Superior and is dotted with natural splendor as well as quaint little towns, shops, old mining relics, and scenic lighthouses. Taking a trip to the Keweenaw is like going back in time.

I have always considered the UP to be a general microcosm of many of the best places I have been. Furthermore, you might say that the Keweenaw is a microcosm of the microcosm. So, one could either take this ambitious day trip; or spend at least a couple overnights up there.

First, we cross the Portage Canal Lift Bridge [244-286 W Lakeshore Drive, Houghton, Michigan 49931; 16TCT8061120097] connecting the twin cities of Houghton and Hancock, then head up a steep, curvy climb on US Highway 41. For your initial stop, take a quick look from the Keweenaw Waterway Scenic Turnout [Hancock, Michigan 49930; 16TCT7999920944]. Here you can see back all the way down the valley.

Quincy Mine

About a half mile further up the road is the old *Quincy Mine* [49750 US Highway 41, Hancock, Michigan 49930; quincymine.com; (906) 482-3101; 16TCT8057221586], which has a distinctive structure. If time permits, it showcases interesting tours of the old, tough days of mining.

Boston Pond Nature Area

Only about 3.5 miles northeast, along US Highway 41, you will come across the Boston Pond Nature Area [51875 US Highway 41, Boston Location Road, Boston, Michigan, 49913; keweenawlandtrust.org; (906) 482-0820; 16TCT8490225068]. The pond itself is essentially a nice lake, ringed with hardwoods; but in my opinion, as I discovered in early October of 2022, the real treat is a sublime display of maples that are around the parking area. If you hit them at peak time, you just might be able to enjoy a view like this:

The maples at the Boston Pond Nature Area

Fall colors of all kinds on the Pond path.

I just like how all the colors in this image totally surround you, and almost give a "live feel" for the hiking path.

Calumet and Mohawk

Continue northeast on US Highway 41 toward Calumet. In Calumet Township, you will see, prominently on the left, *The Last Place on Earth* antique shop [59621 US Highway 41, Phillipsville, Michigan 49805; 16TCT9321537328]. This was another neat excursion back in the day, though it no longer seems to be operating. The Keweenaw itself seems like this, but in a positive way. Continue through Calumet.

As you arrive in Mohawk, I highly recommend that you stop into a tasty little bakery on the right-hand side of US Highway 41. *The Wood'n Spoon* [174 Stanton Avenue, Mohawk, Michigan 49950; woodnspoon.com; (906) 337-2435; 16TCT9629639638], run by Bruce Beaudoin and Gretchen Hein. The fresh baked cookies, fruit pies, jams, etcetera, will definitely leave you with other memories you won't soon forget.

Continue northeast along US Highway 41, and check out the roadside Keweenaw Snow Thermometer [16TDT0159145939], a large yardstick which measures the deep snows that the Keweenaw receives from year to year.

Way back in the tough winter of '78/79, when in Chicago we experienced one of our classic, punitive blizzards, we also had one of the snowiest winters on record-with over 90 inches total for the season. However, that same winter, as vividly indicated on the gauge, the Keweenaw got a whopping, unfathomable 390 inches!!

For optimal color and scenic viewing, simply keep driving. Take a brief detour before the tiny town of Phoenix for the Cliff Cemetery [Cliff Drive, Allouez, Michigan 49805; 16TDT0104747681]. Take the first road (Cliff Drive) to the left (west) after the Snow Thermometer (just over a mile) (16TDT0159547874). Follow Cliff Drive for about 0.2 miles. There is a small sign on the righthand side and a small parking lot (16TDT0126447654). Though, to get across the creek (the west branch of the Eagle River) to the actual cemetery may require an ATV, or similar, vehicle.

At peak time, the color palette will also be impressive; mixed hardwoods painting those hills.

Head back to US Highway 41 and continue northeast through Phoenix to experience the changing hardwoods. Watch quickly for the detour to the right down onto Gay Lac La Belle Road heading toward the Mount Bohemia Ski Resort and the areas around Lac La Belle. (Approximately 9.7 miles from the intersection of US Highway 41 and the north turnoff of M-26 in Phoenix)[16TDT1816152595].

To me, the punch of hardwood color here is as good as it gets, rivaling the power of Baraga County. Take the little roads near Wyoming (just south of the intersection of US Highway 41 and Gay Lac La Belle Road) and take in the splendor of it all.

The side roads near Wyoming and Lac La Belle.

Here you will see hardwoods of every conceivable variety putting on their color coats, with tremendous intensity and pine mixed in for good measure. My experience year after year in early October is driving into a color kaleidoscope that rivals that of any place in our country. It's a sensory overload!

Haven Falls Park and Haven Creek Falls

As you near Lac La Belle, you will want to take a side detour west at the fork-in-the-road [16TDT2304648474] to Haven Falls Park [6280 Gay Lac La Belle Road, Mohawk, Michigan 49950; 16TDT2236648107], another winner in the roadside series. This pleasant little park features picnic tables, strong maple colors, and a nice, tall waterfall with creek below. In my mind, it really exemplifies the very best of autumn.

The waterfall and creek at Haven Creek Falls.

Take time to explore the little side roads around here, for the color scenes are just sublime. Plus, if you are fortunate enough to do this on a weekday, you will probably find respectable solitude.

When you have finished exploring this area, head back out and reconnect with US Highway 41 going east toward Copper Harbor.

Covered Drive (US Highway 41)

Soon we come upon the Covered Drive where, for about 10 miles, you have a great roller coaster effect as you go up and down the road with trees almost connecting overhead:

Along the Covered Drive section of US Highway 41.

If you are part of a group, I recommend that either a passenger in the front seat get video of the effect; or, for those more ambitious, a Go Pro can be attached to top of car. Remember to be careful as there are precious few spots to pull over.

As this culminates, you drop down to the shores of Medora Lake [16TDT2598354503]. Keep heading east and you will pass by the Keweenaw Mountain Lodge and into the terminal point of Copper Harbor.

For those of you who might want that more-ritzy experience, or are in a group, the *Keweenaw Mountain Lodge* [14252 US Highway 41, Copper Harbor, Michigan 49918; keweenamountainlodge.com; (906) 289-4403; 16TDT3140756596] is definitely worth considering. Complete with multiple cabins, golf course, and prime dining hall, you will be in for a nice total experience.

Here, you also have a variety of sites to consider.

About 2 miles east of the Fort Wilkins State Park is a small roadside pull off marking the Beginning of US Highway 41 [Mohawk, Michigan

49950; 16TDT3662057117] as it goes over 1,990 miles all the way down to Miami, Florida.

Copper Harbor

The *Astor House Museum & Antique Shop* [562 Gratiot Street, Copper Harbor, Michigan 49918; minnetonkaresort.com; (906) 289-4449; 16TDT3274857607] located at the Minnetonka resort, preserves some of the Keweenaw's rarest and most unique artifacts, including some copper ingots. The latter will give you a good feel for the denseness of copper.

Now is also a good time for that late lunch at the *Mariner North Resort* [245 Gratiot Street, Copper Harbor, Michigan 49918; manirth.com; (906) 289-4637; 16TDT3302757590]. This is a fun dining spot with tasty burgers, soups, and drinks. Be sure to sample that hearty seafood chowder, long a staple.

Lake Fanny Hooe and Manganese Falls

Prior to your return to Ontonogan, you might want to drive along the shores of Lake Fanny Hooe, via Manganese Road and up the incline to Manganese Falls [9332 Manganese Road, Copper Harbor, Michigan 49918; 16TDT3381156762]. It is less than one mile.

For this waterfall, I generally tend to enjoy and photograph the streams at the top as the waterfall itself drops into a steep canyon and is not easily accessible (therefore, more dangerous as well). You will find a couple of interesting perspectives at the top.

If you are really ambitious, you might want to head to the peaceful Estivant Pines area [a parking lot and trail head is west of Manganese Road on Burma Road; 16TDT3385855113]. The total distance from Copper Harbor is only about 2.5 miles.

The Return to Ontonogan

Brockway Mountain

On the way back down through Copper Harbor, we head west briefly on US Highway 41; but continue west on Gratiot Street instead. As we leave Copper Harbor, make a left onto Brockway Mountain Drive [16TDT3203257777] to climb to the top of Brockway Mountain [Brockway Mountain Drive, Mohawk, Michigan 49950; 16TDT2698257213]. I have found that, over the years, this is a road that really needs to be resurfaced, so, be cautious, and use lower gears as you both climb, and later, descend.

The views in all directions from the top can be quite amazing, including those out into Lake Superior. In fact, if viewing conditions are ideal, you might be able to catch a faint glimpse of Isle Royale, way out in the lake. But don't get too excited; if anything, it's merely a distant image.

A view from the top of Brockway Mountain.

The picture above, looking southwest, shows a sea of color below; and you will also find healthy clusters of aspens straight below the cliffs.

Now, take the slow descent west down the drive. hugging the shores of Lake Upson to your left (south). At the terminal point of Brockway Mountain Drive it will merge with M-26 [16TDT1923757163].

Silver River Falls

Continue west on M-26 and as soon as you cross the bridge over the Silver River (only a matter of several feet), pull into the small parking spaces near the bridge on either the north or south side of the road [16TDT1913657161].

Here you will find the tranquil area of Silver River Falls. Cross the bridge, and head down along the river to view different spots on both sides of the river. You will find it to be pleasant and not overrun with visitors.

Now, the journey back continues as we head west on M-26, hugging the shores of Lake Superior to the north and Lake Bailey to the south. We will pass through the quaint town of Eagle Harbor, getting some nice views of the lake all along.

Eagle Harbor Lighthouse

If time permits, visit the Eagle Harbor Lighthouse [670 Lighthouse Road, Eagle River. Michigan 49950; keweenawhistory.org; 16TDT1262356896]. Take Front Street north to North Street and east to Lighthouse Road.

The Jampot and Jacobs Falls

After you have passed Great Sand Bay, you will come upon another fun, tasty little spot, *The Jampot* [6500 M-26, Eagle Harbor, Michigan 49950; poorrockabbey.com; 16TDT0674053501] which features organic treats in a monastery-owned shop. The, just west of the shop, you will find on the left (south) side of the road, the steep drop of Jacob's Falls [16TDT0667253461]. This is a neat, draping waterfall that can be hiked around and up as well.

Eagle River Falls

Once you arrive in Eagle River, stop at the parking lot on 4th [right before the bridge and across from the Eagle River Museum; 16TDT0219751819] and take a distant look at the drop of Eagle River

Falls [5055 M-26, Eagle River, Michigan 49950; (906) 337-4579; 16TDT0219851754]. You can set up tripod here, but, due to the distance, keep telephoto options open on your gear.

As we conclude the Keweenaw to back where we started, we will turn inland on M-26 to the tiny town of Phoenix where we turn right (west) and are back on US Highway 41 [16TDT0355349179]. The trip from Eagle River to Ontonagon is approximately 80 miles and will take about 1 1/2 hours without any stops.

A view of Eagle River Falls from the Eagle River Historic Bridge.

In summary, the Keweenaw is just loaded with scenic, tasty, and fun possibilities. I think you will find it to be richly rewarding. A place you can return to over and over.

Day 6

For the final full day based out of Ontonogan, we will want to head west along M-64 to the ultimate glory and culmination of the Porcupine Mountains State Park (also known as the Porkies).

However, before reaching the Porkies, we will want to take in a couple sites along M-64. There are many creeks which feed into Lake Superior with colored hardwoods alongside. If conditions are optimal, you might want to take a quick stop to get some pictures.

Bonanza (Iron Creek) Falls

Where M-64 turns inland and begins to head south [16TCS0414589530], just before the Big Iron River, you will want to head a less than a mile down the road to the right (west) at the area of Bonanza Falls (also known as Iron Creek Falls) [16TCS0420288120].

Bonanza Falls

At peak-color time, generally the first week of October, this spot will reward you with the usual suspects: strong river flow with waterfalls around, and that root-beer tannin added in for more color. It can be quite a neat little area to work in and rarely overrun with visitors.

Also, to be noted are those distinctive layers of shale. They create neat handiwork for nature to create multiple waterfalls as they careen down in almost stairstep fashion.

Porcupine Mountain State Park (The Porkies)

Now, travel back up M-64 to the T intersection (16TCS0414589530) and head west on 107th Engineers Memorial Highway toward Porcupine Mountains State Park, one of the only large tract stands of virgin timber left in the Midwest. In fact, at around 31,000 square acres, it is the largest such tract west of the Adirondacks in upstate New York.

In the Fred Bond book I mentioned earlier, in the section on Yosemite National Park, he basically summarized it thusly: "The park is jam packed with spectacular scenery."

In a way, I would say the same for the Porkies: Lake Superior shoreline, waterfalls, stunning overlooks, and those down-the-road vistas which are loaded with magical colors that stem from the multitude of sugar maple, American basswood, eastern hemlock, and yellow birch present in the park.

Concisely put, the Porkies are another one of those amazing UP areas which I would send folks straight to if they want that truncated trip which gives them the best of the autumn experience.

In general, come the first week of October, this is as good a place as any to experience prime fall splendor. For those of you in a more ambitious mood, there are great treks to take into the wilderness for overnight backpacking.

In December 2022, the Porkies received one ranking as "The most beautiful U.S. state park."

Day 7

Keep heading west to the intersection of 107th Engineers Memorial Highway and South Boundary Road (Just over 3 miles from the intersection with M-64) [16TCS0001988304].

Later in the day, we will head right back to this spot, for a magical reason, but for now, let's head south on South Boundary Road to the Porcupine Mountains Visitor Center [33303 Headquarters Road, Ontonagon, Michigan 49953; dnr.state.mi.us; (906) 885-5275; 16TBS9977087949]. You will want to pick up your day passes here.

This is also a nice, informative spot which can also be fun on a rainy day because it has a little theater which tells the story and history of the Porkies, informative rangers, and brochures about all trails and wildlife in the park (and yes, black bears are part of it; so, utilize sensible cautions). This is definitely an educational spot.

Depart the visitor center and continue south on South Boundary Road- as it curves around toward the south/southwest. Be prepared for some stretches of rougher road. At the time of my initial writing in 2019, the initial stretch here was fairly rough. Hopefully, this situation has been rectified.

Along the road, if you hit it just right, the hardwoods will be doing their thing of course; so, if you find little spots to pull off, do so to get more great photographic shots.

We want to head toward the Union Creek area and the Lost Lake Trail. For the latter, watch for the sign for campground on left (south) side of road.

If you have an extra day or two, I recommend taking in large parts of the Union Creek area. It has many interesting, isolated cascades, as well as education: You learn a great deal about copper, and the very difficult days of the 1840s.

The pure willpower of settlers back then, as well as the difficult conditions under which they worked and lived, really puts things into perspective.

For those of you who want a vigorous hike to a nice, isolated mountain lake, the Lost Lake Trail is a good one. It will take you about 1.9 miles to the target and give you some prime isolation. If you are even more daring, doing this early morning on a still day can yield some great autumn reflections.

Summit Peak

Continue on South Boundary Road until the T intersection with Summit Peak Road, on right (north) side of road [16TBS8949978572]. (Approximately 11 miles from the visitors center.)

Take Summit Peak Road to the parking area [16TBS8832980389]. You then take a vigorous uphill climb to the Summit Peak Tower [16TBS8828480867]. From here, you can climb to the top of the tower to get a splendid view of miles and miles of color.

This is kind of a primer for Lake of the Clouds. But remember, we will save the best for last; for later in the day.

Little Carp River and Greenstone Falls

Once back to South Boundary Road, continue west. Our prime target area coming up will be the trails around the Little Carp River and

A classic, down-the-road shot during the hike to the Little Carp River.

Greenstone Falls. At the turnoff for Little Carp River Road [16TBS8358677387], go a short distance down the road to the Little Carp River Parking, on the right [16TBS8383477538]. (Back in the day, the road itself went all the way down to the creek; but now, you simply hike the short distance from the parking lot.)

What I have often liked about this kind of shot, and what it represents: the mixing of green and gold, sort of a symbol of the changing season.

Now, we take a little hike right in along the Little Carp River, making sure to stay parallel with it. Just follow the signs to the little gem of Greenstone Falls [16TBS8358578390].

A footbridge crosses the creek [16TBS8412977917]; so, you might want to incorporate this into your shots as well.

Greenstone Falls, just east of the footbridge.

Overlooked Falls in the Greenstone Area.

Again, the scenic and nature experience possibilities in this area are countless. Make sure to hike along the creek, getting different perspectives. You can even go to Greenstone Falls itself; and for those of you with overnight permits, cabins are available further in to take full advantage.

Return to South Boundary Road and continue to the west.

The Presque Isle River System

Earlier, I mentioned the area of the Black River System and briefly went into some analysis.

That is because this area, Presque Isle, is another one that is jam packed with scenic possibilities of an even higher order. In fact, if time permits, I suggest several hours inside enjoying the total splendor.

To access, continue all the way west to the terminal point of South Boundary Road at Presque Isle Road [Forest Trail 117 / County Road 519; 16TBS7251575636]. One could conceivably take Presque Isle Road south (left) for fine scenery; or, better yet, to the north (right) to access Presque Isle.

Heading north, we will stop at the entrance to see a ranger, if on duty. Then, simply drive up to the first parking area [16TBS7259676680] and get ready for some special hiking.

Since we will be inside here for potentially a couple hours or more, it is advisable to pack your full gear (including water).

Initially, you hike through a pleasant mixed, old-growth forest. This will take you to the top of a terrific wooden-step platform system which accesses the various waterfalls below Presque Isle.

It is interesting to note that, several years back, when my sister and I were hiking here, we all of a sudden heard the telltale sign of a large branch cracking, starting to fall. We simply stopped in our tracks as it crashed to the ground, just barely out of our range! It was large enough to have seriously injured one of us.

Granted, this is a statistically rare case, though, it obviously has to be handled with caution as well. But this is a tough case in which, if you can't see a quick object coming; then, your chances might be as good if you either freeze or run fast.

The Stair Steps

From the top of the platform, you have a choice of which waterfalls to pick. So, for convenience, let's start by going to the right (southeast) all the way down to Nawadaha Falls [16TBS7278075064]. Keep in mind that this is a very good stair system, but can be vigorous to hike as well, so be prepared.

From here, you can walk to the end of the platform to see the power of the river. After strong rainfall, the effect is really something, with mist often blasting to enhance the effect.

I know it's almost becoming a tautology, but at this time of the year, the hardwoods around the river add to the effect.

You could now hike back up the steep staircase, and head just a tad north to Manido Falls [16TBS7292676669].

Manabezho Falls is next heading north [16TBS7284776978]. This is the steepest drop of the 3, at about 25 feet. From the platform, it is best photographed via telephoto.

Manabezho Falls from the observation platform.

At the end point of the platform, you will cross a neat suspension bridge [16TBS7274877069].

Here, as many have done countless times, you will still want to take in the view and feel the power of the Presque Isle River below. Again, as many times as this has been photographed, I can almost never resist the temptation to do so once more and take in the power, as the river fills the shale potholes below, surrounded by changing foliage. Just make sure that everyone is off the bridge, so that the small vibrations don't rock you or your camera!

The Presque Isle River from the Suspension Bridge

Of course, it will be optimal when there has been a lot of rainfall in the days prior; but if not, you can still get a good shot of the complexity of the area. You might also want some vertical shots and videos upstream, as this will further show how the system powerfully moves along.

When you cross the Suspension Bridge to the east side, you are essentially meeting the North-Country Scenic Trail. (See https://northcountrytrail.org/the-trail/trail-map-and-downloads/ for a downloadable map of the North Country Trail) From here, you can detour to the left (north) for nice areas along Lake Superior, including some neat inlets where there are glass-like reflections. You will definitely want to head south along or even in the river, through the pleasant birch forest and get up close to, even inside of, the stone structures. The scenery all around will be very pleasing.

East side trail out towards Lake Superior

In short, plan to take a minimum of several hours in this area. You will be highly rewarded with some of the best, most appetizing natural areas the UP has to offer.

Here, once again, I have to refer to the book by Bond. In a section about another of my favorite areas, Rocky Mountain National Park, what I term the Triple-Lake System: Nymph, Dream, and Emerald Lakes. Paraphrasing what he says:

"This general hike will give you, in the shortest amount of time, a sampling of some of the very best scenery in all the West; almost more than any other area I can think of."

In my estimation about the UP, I would say the same for the Presque Isle River System.

Lake-of-the-Clouds Overlook

In order to access this special place (discussed in the introduction to this section), we simply back track to the point where South Boundary Road begins.

Of course, keep an eye out for deer, as they like this area. You just might see things from a different angle of light now, as you head back.

At the "T" intersection of South Boundary Road with 107th Engineers Memorial Highway [16TCS0001988304], turn left and head west along Lake Superior. You will be making a steep climb; so, be prepared to use lower gears for both the ascent and descent later on. Depending on your timing, there is also a ranger-entry point; but if you are already paid and possess a pass, simply show that to them if they are still present.

There are good trails along this route. If time permits, or you are camping overnight, you might want to check out at least one.

A view from the Lake of the Clouds Overlook

However, our real gem now is the parking area at the top (approximately 7.5 miles from the intersection with South Boundary Road; [16TBS8906786978]. You can walk the nice boardwalk system to at least a couple of marvelous vantage points. At the end, if your timing is just right (around October 5th), then you might be rewarded with a glorious view.

Just splendid, and with still reflections, the scene is pumped up even more. (Although, in my long experience, I have found those to be statistically rare; it is often at least a bit windy up here.)

Year to year, I have discovered that just about no two times has the view or splendor been exactly the same. Slight variations in color and timing occur so that the palette changes. However, near or at peak time it's rarely been a disappointment.

The ideal setting is early evening with the sun setting in the west and a multitude of colors. Of course, even on weekday evenings, with the popularity of this spot, you will probably find heavy crowds. In fact, it sometimes even seems like a photographer's convention.

All should enjoy the spectacle together, peacefully.

Day 8

As we enter the final phase of our trip, our ultimate goal will be the fun area of Munising, in the east, a great baseline from which to launch more of those rewarding mini trips and hikes.

From Ontonagon, you head south on US Highway 45 with the endpoint destination the little town of Rockland (about 12 miles).

Holy Family Cemetery

Enroute, feel free to stop in at the Holy Family Cemetery of Ontonogan on your right (west)[16TCS2369791427]. It is small with a nice historical feel.

An infrared photograph of the Holy Family Cemetery of Ontonogan from 2010.

Of course, in order to achieve an infrared photograph, you will need that special infrared filter and on sunny days, one really picks up a lot of the sun's infrared output.

Old Victoria

Once you arrive in Rockland, turn right (west) on Elm Street [16TCS3350878024] which will turn into Victoria Dam Road as you leave town. You will encounter some steep hills before arriving at the little town of Old Victoria [25401 Victoria Dam Road, Victoria, Michigan 49960; (906) 886-2617; 16TCS2967274577] (about 4 miles west/ southwest).

The tiny village of Old Victoria will definitely give you that throwback feel to those times of old with its remaining structures and schoolhouse. It is also one of the first towns in our country where copper mining occurred. It was originally called Finns Town since a host of mixed European settlers worked and lived here.

You can either take a self-guided walking tour or, if personnel are on site, it's worth hearing their educational talk about these times as well. It is a very fun spot all around, as well as a great place to get some neat photographs.

One of the buildings at Old Victoria

This is also a location where I highly recommend black and white photography or, if you have the gear, the use of infrared. It adds another artistic layer to your work.

A combined black and white and infrared photograph at Old Victoria

Once you have completed your visit of Old Victoria, head back to Rockland to reconnect with US Highway 45, turning right (south) [16TCS3350878024].

Irish Hollow Cemetery

Just after US Highway 45 makes a turn to the east, check out the Irish Hollow Cemetery on you right [16TCS3435277494]. Another small and historical gem.

When US Highway 45 joins with M-26 [16TCS3592277470], turn right (south) and continue on US Highway 45 past a couple of our old friends: the trail to Oh-Kun-de-Kun and Bruce Crossing.

At the intersection with M-28 in Bruce Crossing [16TCS3293555779], turn left (east) and continue past Agate Falls until M-28 merges with US Highway 41 (approximately 38.5 miles)[16TCS8721260132]. Turn right (southeast) on US Highway 41.

As you drive around, don't hesitate to stop and take in more hardwoods; many could be past peek, but if you hit it just right, others will be putting on their glorious coats.

But before this, keep in mind the intersection for FFH 16 again; I will examine the south section of it near the end of this book.

Tioga Creek Roadside Park

As we head farther east on US Highway 41, be sure to stop in at the Tioga Creek Roadside Park, a splendid roadside park (approximately 6.5 miles) [16TCS9733758825].

There are numerous vantage points with good scenes, and if you really explore the trails, you will be delighted at the hidden creek and tiny waterfalls that abound.

For obvious reasons, this makes for a terrific picnic area.

Our real, ultimate goal for the day here, as we pass through Ishpeming and Negaunee, will be the city of Marquette [16TDS6968853849], the largest city in the UP.

For those so inclined, a neat place to visit in Ishpeming is the *U.S. National Ski and Snowboard Hall of Fame* [610 Palms Avenue, Ishpeming, Michigan 49849; skihall.com; (906) 485-6323; 16TDS4893250145].

Why is Marquette our ultimate goal?

Well, not for any of the normal city things, though you might find those useful as well. For example, the many restaurants, and little shops with Scandinavian gifts. However, the Marquette area also boasts some special scenic possibilities.

For those waterfall hunters, of course, this is also a complete area and the one at Morgan Creek is right up there.

To get there takes some doing; so I definitely recommend that fine site again, "gowaterfalling.com" or Phil Stagg's work. The general idea is to take M-553 south of town and take the dirt road toward the Marquette Ski area.

Backlit birch along Tioga Creek

Once, years ago, we did this; and it was tough navigating in a standard car, but, it can be done if great care is taken. Just watch for some rough spots and drive slow.

The end goal is the 20-foot plus drop, which is quite rewarding; and another great spot to hike around.

Wetmore Pond

As more evidence of how the UP, in places, looks downright western, I give you ample evidence to be found at Wetmore Pond.

This unique bog area is like something taken right out of the many, fine mountain lakes out west and seems so tranquil and serene. Come October, the sprinkling of hardwoods around the perimeter and adjacent forests will add to the total experience.

To reach this spot, head about 4.5 miles northwest of Marquette. From US Highway 41 make a left (north) at the traffic circle onto S 7th Street [16TDS6883254121]. Turn left (Northwest) onto Tracy Avenue [16TDS6913756108]. Continue Straight (North) around the traffic circle

View of Wetmore Pond

at Wright Street, Tracy Avenue will turn into Sugar Loaf Avenue. At the T-intersection [16TDS6882057635] turn left (west) onto Big Bay Road (County Road 550). The pull off will be on your left-hand side [16TDS6416961620]; but be very cautious, it comes up kind of suddenly.

You will want to take the main trail through mixed forest and do a little climbing on the rock surfaces. It is very similar to the feel of good hikes out west and the end point will be an amazing viewpoint.

This is essentially a pristine bog habitat and nicely complex, with good viewing platforms. Just be sure to use a little caution around the edges as you don't want to sink in!

Elliott Donelley Wilderness Tract

For those of you seeking even more on County Road 550, head north (about 11 miles northwest of Marquette), and you cross the Little Garlic River. The Elliott Donelley Wilderness Tract [192 Eagles Nest Road, Marquette, Michigan 49855; 16TDS5849869114] will be on your left-hand side.

Take this hike deep into the forest, for various views and sounds around the river. It will also leave you with some great memories, rewarding you with that more isolated experience yet again. Plus, during weekdays, you will have precious little competition.

Presque Isle Park

One of the other treasures of Marquette is Presque Isle Park, a terrific scenic area that hugs Lake Superior and is filled with areas for the sports enthusiast, as well as nature hound.

To get there, take the pleasant Lakeshore Boulevard - which hugs Presque Isle Harbor and takes you to the park. You will pass by some industrial areas; but not to worry, the park opens up into nice treasures.

The main road inside (Peter White Drive) [16TDS7031558800] is one way, so start out and head in an east/northeast (counterclockwise) direction.

Stop at any of the picnic areas and overlooks of Lake Superior before heading to the north shore for the sunset.

If conditions cooperate in this area, you can setup for some memorable scenes over Lake Superior.

The sunset over Lake Superior form Presque Isle

We now head back down the pleasant Lakeshore Boulevard and through the nice waterfront and marina area to its conclusion back at South Front Street (US Highway 41/M-28 east; 16TDS6959853453].

As you leave Marquette, M-28 will break off from US Highway 41 to the left [16TDS7314548202]. Continue to follow M-28 and head east along Lake Superior where little shore parks crop up and provide good stops to relax.

Scott Falls

About 32 miles east, just past the tiny area of Au Train, and right off the road on the right you will find a tiny waterfall, Scott Falls, which is across M-28 from Scott Falls Roadside Park [16TES1405842622].

It's worth a quick look and if you are feeling lazy, can even be done right from your car. It's one of those I term a "bowl waterfall" because it appears to drop into a bowl. You can hike behind and above it as well.

Continue traveling east for about another seven miles to the tiny town of Christmas, which boasts of another fun casino - the *Kewadin Casino* [N7761 Candy Cane Lane, Christmas, Michigan 49862; kewandin.com; (906) 387-5475; 16TES2253042676], if you are so inclined.

Continuing on past Christmas, we approach the baseline for the final leg of our splendid journey, the neat town of Munising [16TES2690539647].

Day 9

Munsing

Munising is a town that is full of potential activities: little restaurants, Garden Bay Winery, and waterfalls even in town. It is also the gateway to Pictured Rocks National Seashore.

There is a large variety of lodging opportunities to suit every desire or pocketbook. A couple of my own favorites over the years have been the *Alger Falls Motel* [E9427 M-28, Munsing, Michigan 49862; algerfallsmotel.com; (906) 387-3536; 16TES2848336672] and the *Terrace Motel* [420 Prospect Street, Munsing, Michigan 49862; exploringthenorth.com; (906) 387-2735; 16TES2671638985] which has an adjacent building with a pool table and other games. We have recently enjoyed the *White Pine Lodge* back in Christmas [E7889 M-28, Christmas. Michigan 49862; whitepinelodgeonline.com; (906) 387-1111; 16TES2229542750]. Good lodging with a large, heated pool and right by the Kewadin Casino.

Eastern UP

It's about 60 miles east along M-28 to the town of Newberry. Much of this route parallels the Soo Line Railroad and passes through the Great Manistique Swamp, so keep your eyes peeled for more photographic possibilities.

Tahquamenon Falls State Park

From Newberry, we will take M-123 [Newberry Avenue/Falls Road; 16TFS1478128843] north/northeast, about 28 miles to the gem of Tahquamenon Falls State Park. Needless to say, this stretch is also lined with some pretty amazing hardwoods on both sides of the road.

The day-use fee for out-of-state visitors to the park as of 2022 was $9 per day, and well worth it. It will give you liberal access to both the upper falls [16TFS3391059839] and lower falls [16TFS3777862796] areas.

If at all possible, try this popular park on a weekday. Even so, especially in recent years, it can get quite crowded, but it's still a fun area. The village itself has nice shops and a tasty brewery. So, be sure to stop in here either before or after your visit to the upper falls.

The walk through the forest to the various views of the falls is ultra pleasant, passing through mixed hardwoods and eastern hemlock. It's quite educational as well.

A viewpoint of Tahquamenon Upper Falls

This is a bit of a telephoto shot, and it gives a feel for the power of the falls. The drop is about 50 feet; and has that neat "root beer" look to it-caused by tannins in the river.

Keep hiking around the top, then down the staircase to the top where you can feel a great combination of power, noise, and mist.

Back at the parking lot, you can either drive about 4 miles downstream (northeast) to the lower falls; or if you make it more a full-day commitment, you can actually hike that distance.

This area is richly rewarding.

Other areas around here which are worth strong mention are the Great Lakes Shipwreck Museum further north at Whitefish Point [18335 North Whitefish Point Road, Paradise, Michigan 49768; shipwreckmuseum.com; (906) 492-3747; 16TFS5589081697] There is information regarding the Edmund Fitzgerald here, plus you get to pass through Paradise (Paradise, Michigan that is). Whitefish Point is approximately 22 miles from Tahquamenon Falls State Park.

The farthest point east is the Soo Locks at Sault Ste. Marie [16TGS0352152823], about 73 miles further from the park. If you were based further down in the direction of the Mackinac Bridge [16TFR7653976525] and Mackinac Island [16TFR8415181559], Lake Huron would be another of the great lakes to explore.

If you were based out of Newberry, you would be able to do these more reasonably, but for our current purposes, I mention them as more tasty temptations for a return trip.

The Seney Ponds

As we head back down through Newberry to M-28, we will backtrack and head west to the junction with M-77 [16TES8032432967]. Our first stop will be south on M-77 about 5 miles to the Seney Ponds National Wildlife Refuge area [16TES8262325816].

Not only is this area a good one for wildlife spotting, in particular, large birds; but it also can be special for still reflections. You will want to take

Wonderful colors of the larch trees at the Seney Ponds National Wildlife Refuge

the self-guiding auto tour, which goes one way. Just go slow and use care.

Pictured Rocks National Seashore

This area is loaded with numerous possibilities, a couple of which we will touch upon for our final day. For now, however, let's backtrack for our last gem of the day.

Head back up north on M-77 to the intersection of M-28 [16TES8032432967]. We continue north on M-77 about 25 miles, to the eastern part of Pictured Rocks.

Once again, this stretch has several areas of clustered hardwoods which can put on quite a show.

Grand Marais

Our first goal is the little town of Grand Marais. From here, briefly head west on Carlson Street/H-58 [16TES7764269197] which is the main road through Pictured Rocks

You might also want to have a cellphone or laptop at your fingertips to access the government website, as it is a national park or national scenic area. This will give more detailed information about roads, weather, and area. (https://www.nps.gov/piro/index.htm)

Sable Falls

About a mile is the parking lot for Sable Falls. [Sable Falls Road turns off to the right as H-58 curves south; 16TES7576168751]

This waterfall area is another of my favorites. The general lack of crowds for such a nice area and strong waterfall are the main reasons.

The hike to the falls will require a little effort as you have to go down a steep platform. You will want to get some intimate views, mostly vertical shots.

Continue to check out the canyon around the stream and the dunes-as they work their way into Lake Superior. This is definitely another award winner.

Anyhow, welcome to Sable:

Sable Falls

Once you have finished exploring Sable Falls and the surrounding area, we continue on to enjoy the features inside Pictured Rocks.

I highly recommend passing by Grand Sable Lake and visiting the area of the Grand Sable Dunes. Try and get to the overlook [16TES7355466579] for these massive structures as they tower about 500 feet above Lake Superior.

As with many of the steep dunes which hug lakes Michigan and Superior, written warnings go out to those hikers attempting them: tough going down, but even tougher, more demanding coming back up.

Therefore, if you or your group does attempt them, be sure that you have the required level of cardio fitness and water as well; for, you would not want to be part of any rescue operation which you would have to ultimately end up paying for.

Also fascinating here is the posted sign about the loggers who worked in the area, back in the late 1800s. A couple of stories about the toils, even tragic deaths in particular, are quite haunting and heart breaking.

As you head back along H-58, keep an eye out for possible sunset spots. Catching glimpses of them over Lake Superior continues to reward. Though we will pass by some important sites, fear not; for, tomorrow we will hit some of these with more time put in.

Ultimately, after about 49 miles total from Grand Marais, we get back to Munising as we prepare for our final, full day.

Day 10

On the final full day devoted to exploring, there are again a multitude of possibilities. Fortunately, many are very close to the Munising area, with one exception.

Schoolcraft County

To get there, we want to head east on M-28/M-94. At Shingleton [16TES4078032850], turn right onto M-94 south, taking in the splendor of Schoolcraft County.

If colors are bursting, you might want to take a brief detour to Colwell Lake on the left-hand (east) side (approximately 9 miles from Shingleton) [16TES4245819356]. If you arrive here in the early morning, you can often get some amazing autumn reflections.

Continue heading south on M-94 all the way down to the Manistique area (approximately 26 miles). Turn right (west) on US Route 2 [16TER5852589090] to M-149 [16TER5204583838] north toward Indian Lake (approximately 5.5 miles). This route gives an interesting tour of the general area. Another way would be to simply take County Highway 442 (Deer Street) west off of M-94 [16TER5683290231], though, it is not as smooth as the US Route 2 to M-149 route. Indian Lake State Park [8970 County Hwy 442, Manistique, Michigan 49854; www.michigandnr.com; (906)341-2355; 16TER5170188082]

A nice little stop is *Linda's Bread Box and Sporting Goods* [10N State Highway M-149, Cooks, Michigan; (906) 644-2284; 16TER4603789208] It has tasty snacks, drinks, and souvenirs.

Palms Book State Park

From *Linda's Bread Box* (at the intersection of Country Highway 442 and M-149) continue north on M-149. Our main goal is Palms Book State Park [michigannr.com; (906) 341-2355; 16TER4774094788] home to one of the neatest scenic treats you will ever come across, Kitch-iti-kipi [16TER4785694696].

On the trail, you will also come across another classic piece, with a powerful reminder about nature itself, *Prayer of the Woods*.

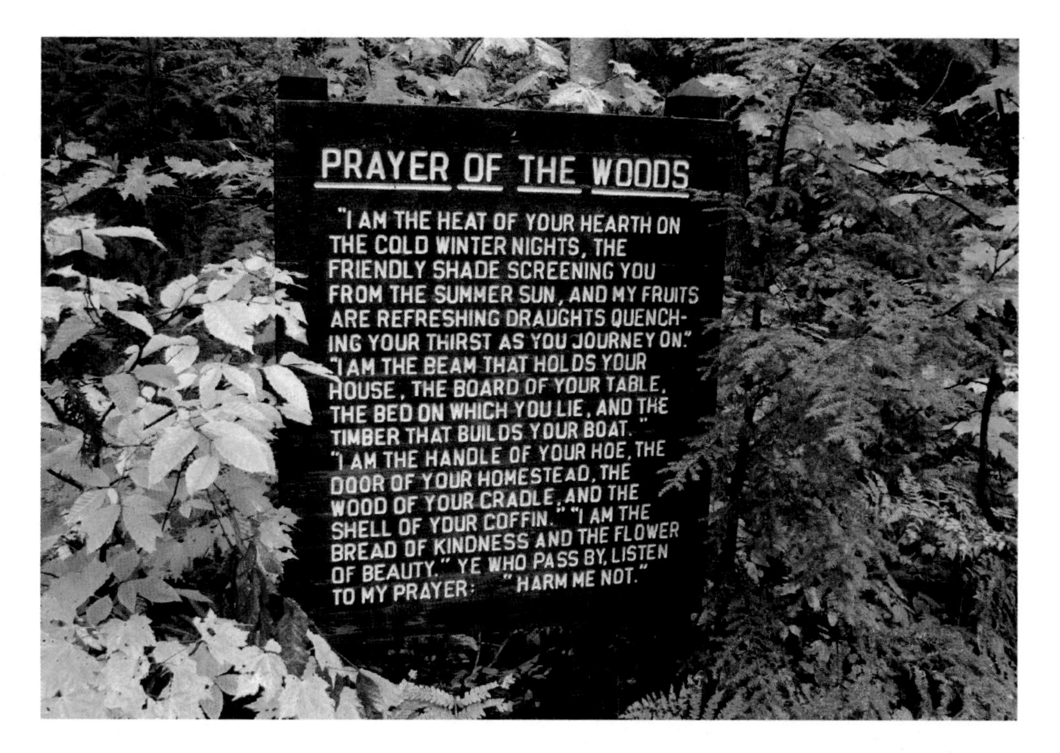

Kitch-iti-kipi

Keep walking and hidden in the forest you will come upon an absolute gem: the still little natural spring, known as "Kitch-iti-kipi", or "The Mirror of Heaven" as the Native Americans termed it.

This is essentially the state's largest freshwater spring and many gallons are pumped into the stunning pool year around at an almost-constant temperature of 45 degrees Fahrenheit.

A self-observation raft that one can pull by cables is provided and takes you and others across this still structure, allowing you to see the emerald bottom, with several kinds of trout included. Come early October, you will also find those golden larches ringing the perimeter.

In addition, a sign talks about the wealthy Bellaire family doing a great thing by setting aside this natural wonder, saving it from neglect in the 1920s for generations to come.

I highly recommend this peaceful gem.

Kitch-iti-kipi

Following your visit to Palms Book State Park and Kitch-iti-kipi, double back to Munising (about an hour drive) and take time to discover the variety of local, simple waterfalls to explore.

Alger Falls

Right off the highway at the junction of M-28 and M-94 [16TES27056377785], you will find the steep drop of Alger Falls. Most of the time, it's a thin waterfall and rather dangerous to access; so, pull well off the road as much as you can, in the small dirt area.

Michigan Nature Association (Olson) Memorial Falls

Another almost-hidden-gem in town is the Michigan Nature Association Memorial Falls (https://gowaterfalling.com/waterfalls/mna.shtml). This site includes a secluded hike through rich forest into a bowl-shaped canyon with sand left over from the history of the lake receding. Head east on H-58 and turn right (south) on Nestor Street [16TES2871740781]. Carefully look for the little hiking sign on the right.

Michigan Nature Association Memorial Falls

Another unique thing about these falls is the cave behind it; it makes for more good images and videos.

Tannery Falls

You can also hike through this area to reach Tannery Falls [https://gowaterfalling.com/waterfalls/tannery.shtml; 16TES2865840281] which is essentially at the end of the street where you park, on the west side. Though, it seems like you have to cross a little private property to access it.

Another way to reach Tannery Falls is to follow the stairs and trail on the south side of M-58 across the street from the Washington Street turnoff [16TES2843640428]. (Do not park on H-58 or you will be ticketed.) Current parking for Tannery Falls is onstreet parking on Cleveland Street (Off of Nestor Street).

It is worth the effort. Here at Tannery Falls you will find a winning waterfall that is essentially a twin drop. Be careful of the steep terrain.

Wagner Falls

The real gem in this compact area, however, is Wagner Falls, which is actually a state scenic site. Turn off of M-28 onto M-94 (by Alger Falls) [16TES2702637804]. There is a parking lot located on the left (south side of the road just as M-94 curves to the west) [16TES2698437326]. Be careful here, as the high-speed traffic from both highways comes together suddenly.

This splendid area features an easy boardwalk hike through rich forest, creeks, and terminates with the platform view of Wagner Falls. For the most part, you will probably end up with vertical shots and videos; though, I often like working in the stream below. Either way, you can't go wrong.

For even more fun and an improved treat, hike up above the standard viewing spot, back through the forest, and follow Wagner Creek to its many tributaries and cascades. This will give you more isolation, but also great waterfall possibilities as well.

You will generally find this section also has fewer total visitors.

Wagner Falls

Upper Peninsula Inspired Winery

Upper Peninsula Inspired Winery [321 East Superior Street, Munising, Michigan 49862; (906) 387-1387; 16TES2682139579] is a tasty little spot that makes for an excellent visit in any weather of course, but particularly so on a rainy day. Though, quite honestly, if we take lunch about now, I highly recommend this no matter what the weather.

Formerly the Garden Bay Winery (now located in Cooks, Michigan), this outlet still carries wines from that winery- as well as four other wineries within the state, along with a shop of tasty morsels. (And it also carries wines and meads from another of my favorites, Threefold Vine.) For those like myself with that sweet palette, one of my personal favorites is Old Mack Peach and Honey. It's definitely very sweet and has those tastes nicely represented and mirrored.

Miners Castle Rock

As the "final punch" for our last full day, we will want to end things with a couple very-special spots inside of Pictured Rocks.

Head east on County Road H-58 (Adams Trail) once more for approximately 5 miles, toward the intersection of Miners Castle Road [16TES3435040777] which leads to the classic overlook of Miners Castle Rock, a terrific scenic and educational spot. So, we will want to take Miners Castle Road north to its terminal point, about 5 miles [16TES3448349001].

It's almost become a tautology at this point again, but this road is yet another which, generally as October advances more (past the 5th), has splendid colors on both sides.

If you are spending more days in this area, Miners Falls is highly recommended. Turn off of Miners Castle Road onto Miners Falls Road [16TES3431646769] to reach the parking area and trailhead [16TES3509746823]. It involves a vigorous one-mile hike, with a view of a stunning drop [16TES3600146894]. If you hit it after a hard rain, like I did a couple of times, the power and the mist will be quite impressive. You can also work the area around, and on top of, Miners Falls, but be very cautious; the canyon is steep, and footing can be challenging.

From the parking area at Miners Castle Point, follow the path to the Upper Overlook to simply contemplate the excellent view of Miners Castle Rock and Lake Superior.

Miners Castle Rock from the Upper Overlook

Given different times and lighting, you can see shades of greens, but also blues in the water-that almost look like a scene out of the South Pacific. As shown, many birch trees cling to the canyon, adding to the color show.

Take time to hike around at the top and take in a view of Grand Island, the castle itself, and the beach below.

If you are looking for even more fun adventures, check out the glass-bottom boat tours - *Glass Bottom Shipwreck Tours* [1204 Commercial Street #1354, Munising, Michigan 49862; shipwrecktours.com; (906) 387-4477; 16TES2601841209], the Pictured Rocks boat tours - *Pictured Rock Cruises, LLC* [100 City Park Drive, Munising, Michigan 49862; picturedrocks.com; (906) 387-2379; 16TES2654139957], or take in the action "first hand" as you kayak around these stunning waters and cliffs - *Pictured Rocks Kayaking* [1348 Commercial Street, Munising, Michigan 49862; paddlepicturedrocks.com; (906) 387-5500; 16TES2633841562].

Each is truly rewarding on so many levels. One example of the scenes on the boat tour which you just can't see as well, or at all, on land, is the East Channel Lighthouse on Grand Island, with colors popping.

The East Channel Lighthouse on Grand Island

Chapel Falls And Mosquito Falls

You can also head further east on H-58 and take in Chapel Falls [Section Thirty-Four Creek, Shingleton, Michigan 49884; 16TES4262652952] or the more isolated Mosquito Falls [Mosquito River, Shingleton, Michigan, 49884; 16TES4005051544]. Both are worth the visit.

Munising Falls

For our last act, we want to end the day at the splendid and easy-to-access area of Munising Falls [1505 Sand Point Road, Munising, Michigan 49862; www.nps.gov; (906) 387-4310; 16TES2885841188] conveniently located almost within town. On a return via H-58, turn right (north) on Washington Street [16TES2842540436] essentially going northeast into the Pictured Rocks area (the sign for this will be obvious.) Though, even further down this road, you will also find the interesting area of Sand Point which features a bog area that is also Western looking.

Munising Falls Creek and the wooden foot bridge

From the parking lot, you can visit the small national park visitor center and walk through a pleasant creek-in-forest. You can even do some photographing around the creek, almost in it, in fact.

You will come upon a wooden bridge that takes you to the steep drop of the falls, nestled nicely in a canyon. If you hit this after strong rainfalls, the effect is, of course, greatly magnified.

The real gem is the flow of the creek around that wooden bridge, looking toward the falls- which kind of represents a classic autumn feel

This is yet another area in which you should completely immerse yourself in the sites, sounds, and aroma. To me, it is, on a compact scale, the exemplification of fall.

Exit Strategy

As you depart from Munising, you will want to (weather permitting) take in the area of Cox Pond. You can park at the Robert McQuisten Recreation Area [Conners Road; www.munisingtownship.org; (906) 387-4404; 16TES2948636129] to access a wonderful boardwalk system over the bog, and if the colors are right on, you can get both good mixes and reflections. Take M-28/M-94 south of town into Wetmore. Turn right (South) on Conners Road (NF-13) [16TES2958336492] for 0.2 of a mile. The parking area is on the right (west).

The colors along the road to Powell Lake

Utilize NF-13 on your 40-mile tour south. This journey is a prime cut through the Hiawatha National Forest and you will find maximum color punch generally, as October moves along; around October 7th and later.

It therefore features strong autumn scenery with powerful colors, hidden lakes, deep forest roads, and mixes of colors in pines.

You will find various scenes like this along the route with both the color and geometry which will give you some interesting, artistic perspectives to enjoy and photograph. Just one of many examples is the detour to Powell Lake.

As you move further south, toward the end of NF-13, you might want to check out Pete's Lake [Inwood Township, Michigan; 16TES3086819267], Wishing Well Springs, and the larch trees that start to turn brilliant gold. They will top off another nice, complex scenic experience.

Finale

As we end our journey on NF-13, it intersects with US Route 2 (16TER2285782465). From here you can work your way west, going through a solid chunk of Delta County.

If you have additional time, approximately 86 miles east on US Route 2 is the neat Cut River Bridge and roadside park (16TFS4525800645) just east of Epoufette. When ringed by autumn colors, it's also quite a site.

For those of you with added interest in exploring, Garden Peninsula, which extends about 22 miles south of US Route 2 on 183, is recommended.

Fayette Historic State Park

Fayette Historic State Park [4785 II Road, Garden , Michigan 49835; dnr.state.mi.us; (906) 644-2603; 16TER2587462684] is one big winner there, situated along Big Bay de Noc. Loaded with history and an old, quaint little village, it is a scenic and educational area. There is a real feel of going back in time here with an old schoolhouse and other structures that were part of the 1860s.

Fishing for many varieties is also plentiful here. Plus, sample some of the stores for prime cherry products. Not only the berries themselves, but tart cherry juice concentrate is available.

It all makes for a scenic, tasty experience in its own right.

Days River Area

Continue heading west on US Route 2, until the merger with US Highway 41 (United Spanish War Veterans Memorial Highway) [16TER0195885901], and continue south. North of Escanaba, keep your eyes peeled for Days River 24.5 Road [16TDR9975181920]- which is just south of 255 Lane. It comes up kind of quick on the west side of the road. Turn right (west) and follow it for 2.5 miles

On the way, you will pass a tiny, old village and schoolhouse [16TDR9848881958]. Follow the road around the golf course and stop at the Days River Trailhead [6310 Days River 24.5 Road, Gladstone, Michigan 79837; (906) 786-2351; 16TDR9635681846], on the right (north).

A scene from the Days River Trailhead

This is a short hike, but features character and hardwoods all its own that justify the detour. On the pleasant walk down to the river, you will notice an excellent, lined geometry of trees.

You will also find nice vertical arrangements. So, immerse yourself in this peaceful area. Also take the short hike across the river, via the bridge. Here you also have a splendid mixed forest.

Finale Points

Now, head back out and continue south through the town of Escanaba, another of the UP's largest. Depending on the nature of your trip, this could be a good place to stay as well. It has numerous restaurants, stores, and services for just about anything.

From here, we can take M-35 south, as it splits from US Highway 41 as it hugs Lake Michigan, before dropping down into Wisconsin, passing through Menominee, Michigan and Marinette, Wisconsin. There are several good examples of parks to stop at. J.W. Wells State Park [7670 M-35, Stephenson, Michigan 49887; dnr.state.mi.us; (906) 863-9747; 16TDR7124226943] is just one prime example for exploration.

On a nice autumn day, it creates another peaceful, idyllic setting:

A scene of the colors at the J. W. Wells State Park

There are also two other good wineries.

Threefold Vine Winery

Perhaps my favorite winery in the UP is the *Threefold Vine Winery* [S232 Menominee Street, Stephenson, Michigan 49887; exploringthenorth.com; (906) 753-6000; 16TDR5230929257], in the historical little town of Stephenson. To access it, you can either go south from Escanaba on M-35 (as described), then just past Cedar River, travel west on County Road 352 G12; or west from Escanaba via US Route 2 / US Highway 41, then south US Highway 41 south all the way to Stephenson. Threefold Vine Winery is embedded inside an old bank; you almost can't tell that's what it is, but Jan is a fun host and the variety of meads in particular are some of the very best I have had, because they straddle the sweet and tart line amazingly.

Yooper Winery

In Menominee, I highly recommend a stop in at John Lucas's *Yooper Winery* [915 48th Avenue, Menominee, Michigan 49858; yooperwinery.com; (906) 864-9302; 16TDQ5193299094] This is another fun winery. It also features great variety, especially for those with sweet palettes and John is a very entertaining host and proprietor. Just a couple of examples are that Old Mack Honey Peach (which Upper Peninsula Inspired in Munising does carry, as mentioned), and Red Currant. They are sweet, smooth, and quite tasty.

Backtracking and Alternate Route

If we choose not go this way, however, we can continue along US Highway 41 / US Route 2 west, out of Escanaba and continue on US Route 2 west to where it intersects with US Highway 8 [16TDR2927670817] at the tiny town of Norway, approximately 43 miles.

Fumee Falls

Approximately 3.5 miles farther west on US Route 2, on the north side of the road, just before the tiny town of Quinnesec, is another little waterfall gem, clearly visible from the road itself: Fumee Falls, located at the Fumee Creek Roadside Park [US Route 2, Quinnesec, Michigan 49876; 16TDR2396272965]. This is neat little place to explore, with modern platform and benches. You can also go up and to the side of the falls. One real treat about this area: It is pretty easy to both observe and navigate.

The Pasty Oven

Whether or not you are coming from the east or west along US Route 2 (see below), I definitely recommend the little eatery *The Pasty Oven* [W7279 Highway, US Route 2, Quinnesec, Michigan 49876; pastys.com; (906) 776-0990; 16TDR231572958]. Here you will find a variety of simple foods, but most of all, those tasty pasties I mentioned early in the book. You really have to treat yourself to at least one.

Federal Forest Highway 16/NF-16, Part II

As I mentioned earlier, in the section of NF-16/FFH 16 (Page 59), we would return to the second part as it drops south of M-28 [16TCS5470649777], well over 20 miles to its intersection with US Route 2 [16TCS5489413562].

If you do a truncated trip; for example, staying over in the western sections only, I highly recommend this adventure as well. The prime time is generally around October 1 (though, in a year that is lagging a bit, several days later will also work.)

Much like the north section, this is also a prime cut through the Ottawa National Forest and with it of course comes a multitude of hardwood colors.

The beautiful hardwoods of the Ottawa National Forest

Here, we even have a little of that snow mixed in, which can happen as October moves along.

Then at US Route 2 east, you eventually hit Larsen again.:

A nice autumn setting

Back on M-95 South

As mentioned at the beginning of this book, if you are on a truncated trip, and leave on US Highway 41 east, going south on M-95 (Leif Erickson Memorial Highway) is another option. The drive has interesting topography all its own, often with nice areas of those aspens and larch.

The aspen and larch along M-95.

Our Final Stop – Piers Gorge Scenic Hiking Trail

Before my closing remarks, and as I stated early in this book, we now come to our final scenic stop, the Piers Gorge Scenic Hiking Trail [Piers Gorge Road, Norway, Michigan 49870; dnr.state.mi.us; (906) 563-9247; 16TDR2676467718], which is right on the Michigan/Wisconsin border, with the power of the Menominee River very much on display.

Generally, late in the first week of October is a solid bet on color punch and if you go October 5th and later, you should be in good shape.

This is just south of Norway, Michigan on US Highway 8, west side of the highway with sign indicating the area via Piers Gorge Road [16TDR2841468003].

You will want to head west about a mile, and park at the designated area [16TDR2676467718]. There is a $9 fee for day use (unless you have a more general pass), but it's more than worth the cost.

On an alternate trip, to wet your palette, you can also join a rafting team. There is an outfit for this not far from US-8, and on the Piers Gorge Road, *Tarka's Whitewater Journey* (W6046 Piers Gorge Road, Norway, Michigan 49870; www.whitewaterjourney,com). This will give you an added layer of fun.

I like this entire area because it another of those great little microcosms: complex, changing forests, boulders, rapid waters that create waterfalls, and dramatic overlooks. If you are fortunate enough to experience this after rain has come through, you will get not only stronger water flow; but that great aroma of the changing forests of autumn.

The first part is almost tropical with little streams and ferns, plus a boardwalk over the creek. It then changes to mixed hardwoods and finally, the various piers or waterfalls open up to hike to for dramatic looks down to the river, like so:

The Menominee River from the Piers Gorge Scenic Trail

From this vantage point, high above the river, you are looking southwest down toward some powerful waterfall action as the river forms the borderline of the states, plus, those great hardwood colors are very much on display.

Take the necessary time in this area and even go west to the multiple piers; it is truly rewarding.

Conclusion

Now you have come to the end of your journey.

In real time, you may be heading back through Wisconsin or, perhaps to another part of the country. But I hope you are absorbing and reflecting on the magnitude of it all and considering a repeat trip or exploring additional areas of Michigan's Upper Peninsula, for it is an amazing place loaded with scenic grandeur, especially in the autumn.

It is economical, more isolated, has nice folks, and unique tastes as well.

We live in a world dominated by endless electronic distractions which seem to never let up, barely giving us a moment of reprieve. I therefore think such escapes are more important than ever to basically give us energy, and ultimately, replenish the soul. The autumn experience of nature takes this to the highest level. In my estimation, it is one of the finest experiences that a human can have.

In closing, when talking about visiting the UP in early autumn, I tend to think of a powerful line (one word actually) that a now-retired Chicago police-officer friend of ours, Bob Nichol, once told me at the service for my mom back in late 2013.

Years earlier, he and his wife went to the amazing islands of Fiji for their honeymoon. Knowing that this amazing place was already on my future list as well, I asked him to give it to me straight, asking how it really was.

He paused for about 5 seconds and then told me one word, quite emphatically:

GO!

I would simply say...total, 100% on this for the UP as well. More than any words or photos I can share with you, I recommend getting out into the field and doing it. There is just no substitute for exploring in person and experiencing exactly what we have been discussing in all the prior material.

It just may leave you with some of the best memories of a lifetime.

Appendix

You can see further examples of my work at the following:

https://fineartamerica.com/profiles/collins-robert

Weekly on Craigslist, in the Arts & Craft section for Sales (in Chicagoland, Kalamazoo, and Kenosha) ... Colorful, Sharp, Core Nature-Photo Matted/Canvas/Metal-Print Artwork

Facebook: Bob Collins (Digital Creator)

Instagram: Velvia1967

References within the Book

Westward Ho: Through the Scenic West, by Fred Bond (Cuneo Press) – https://www.amazon.com/Westward-Ho-Through-Scenic-West/dp/B000GWV9WA – Page 12

Fall Colors Across North America, by Anthony E. Cook (Graphic Arts Books) – https://www.amazon.com/Fall-Colors-Across-North-America/dp/1558685995 – Page 12

Pacific Northwest Hiking, by Ron C. Judd and Dan A. Nelson (Foghorn Press) – https://www.amazon.com/Pacific-Northwest-Hiking-Complete-Washington/dp/0935701125 – Page 17

Fun in the UP – https://funintheup.com/ – Page 23, 24

The Upper Peninsula – https://www.uptravel.com/ – Page 23, 29

Michigan Department of Transportation's website – michigan.gov/mdot – Page 28

Department of Natural Resources – Michigan State Parks - https://www.michigan.gov/dnr/places/state-parks – Page 28

Hiking Michigan by Roger E. Storm and Susan M. Wedzel, 1997 edition; but updated in 2009 – Page 48

North Country Trail downloadable map - https://northcountrytrail.org/the-trail/trail-map-and-downloads/ - Page 93

www.Gowaterfalling.com – Page 100, 115, 116

https://www.nps.gov/piro/index.htm – Page 109

Location Index

Major Intersection and Way Point Index

Made in the USA
Monee, IL
14 July 2023

39266903R00088